DON QUIXOTE

Miguel de Cervantes

This edition published by Spark Publishing

Spark Publishing
A Division of SparkNotes LLC
120 Fifth Avenue, 8th Floor
New York, NY 10011

Please submit all comments and questions or report errors to www.sparknotes.com/errors

Printed and bound in the United States

ISBN 1-58663-395-3

CONTENTS

NOTE: This SparkNote refers to the Penguin Classics edition of *Don Quixote,* translated from the Spanish by J. M. Cohen and first published in 1950.

Context

MIGUEL DE CERVANTES SAAVEDRA WAS BORN IN 1547 to a poor Spanish doctor. He joined the army at twenty-one and fought against Turkey at sea and Italy on land. In 1575, pirates kidnapped Cervantes and his brother and sold them as slaves to the Moors, the longtime Muslim enemies of Catholic Spain. Cervantes ended up in Algiers. He attempted to escape his enslavement three times and was eventually ransomed in 1580 and returned to Spain.

Only with the publication of the first volume of *Don Quixote,* in 1604, did Cervantes achieve financial success and popular renown. *Don Quixote* became an instant success, and its popularity even spawned an unauthorized sequel by a writer who used the name Avellaneda. This sequel appeared several years after the original volume, and it inspired Cervantes to hurry along his own second volume, which he published in 1614. Cervantes died the following year, in 1615.

Many of *Don Quixote*'s recurring elements are drawn from Cervantes's life: the presence of Algerian pirates on the Spanish coast, the exile of the enemy Moors, the frustrated prisoners whose failed escape attempts cost them dearly, the disheartening battles displaying Spanish courage in the face of plain defeat, and even the ruthless ruler of Algiers. Cervantes's biases pervade the novel as well, most notably in the form of a mistrust of foreigners.

Funded by silver and gold pouring in from its American colonies, Spain was at the height of its European domination during Cervantes's life. But Spain also suffered some of its most crippling defeats during this time, including the crushing of its seemingly invincible armada by the English in 1588. The tale of the captive, which begins in Chapter XXXIX of the First Part of *Don Quixote,* recounts in detail many of the historical battles in which Cervantes himself participated. In this sense, *Don Quixote* is very much a historical novel.

Nevertheless, the novel illustrates Spain's divergent worlds. Spain at the time was caught in the tumult of a new age, and Cervantes tried to create in *Don Quixote* a place to discuss human identity, morality, and art within this ever-shifting time. Though the Renaissance gave rise to a new humanism in European literature, popular writing continued to be dominated by romances about knights in shining armor practicing the code of chivalry. Chivalry emphasized the protection of the weak, idealized women, and celebrated the role of the wandering knight, who traveled from place to place performing good deeds. Books of chivalry tended to contain melodramatic, fantastical stories about encounters with cruel giants, rescues of princesses in distress, and battles with evil enchanters—highly stylized accounts of shallow characters playing out age-old dramas.

On one level, the first volume of *Don Quixote* is a parody of the romances of Cervantes's time. Don Quixote rides out like any other knight-errant, searching for the same principles and goals and engaging in similar battles. During these battles, he invokes chivalric ideals, regardless of how ridiculous his adventures may be. On another level, however, the adventures of Don Quixote and Sancho Panza in the novel's First Part attempt to describe a code of honor that could serve as an example for a Spain that was confused by war and by its own technological and social successes. Cervantes applies this code of values to a world in which such values are out of date.

In the Second Part, however, Cervantes provides the answer to questions about identity and codes of conduct in the personalities of Don Quixote and especially his sidekick, Sancho Panza. The Second Part is a textured work with responsive and credible characters who engage one another in sincere and meaningful ways. Cervantes wanted to place his novel within a literary tradition that was fluctuating at the time, and the novel's numerous discussions of playwriting, poetry, and literature mark this effort to understand the changes in the intellectual environment.

Cervantes also includes social and religious commentary in *Don Quixote*. He bitterly criticizes the class structure in Spain, where outmoded concepts of nobility and property prevailed even as education became more widespread among the lower classes. The arrogance of the Duke and the Duchess in the Second Part highlights how unacceptable Cervantes found these class distinctions to be. Likewise, the prevailing of Sancho and Teresa Panza's wisdom at the end of the novel is a victory for old-fashioned goodness and wisdom in the face of a world that makes people practical but petty. Finally, Cervantes, who was briefly excommunicated from the Catholic church in 1587, discusses the church in the novel as well. Sancho's self-identification as an "old Christian," in particular, informs the new morality he represents.

Plot Overview

DON QUIXOTE IS A MIDDLE-AGED GENTLEMAN FROM the region of La Mancha in central Spain. Obsessed with the chivalrous ideals touted in books he has read, he decides to take up his lance and sword to defend the helpless and destroy the wicked. After a first failed adventure, he sets out on a second one with a somewhat befuddled laborer named Sancho Panza, whom he has persuaded to accompany him as his faithful squire. In return for Sancho's services, Don Quixote promises to make Sancho the wealthy governor of an isle. On his horse, Rocinante, a barn nag well past his prime, Don Quixote rides the roads of Spain in search of glory and grand adventure. He gives up food, shelter, and comfort, all in the name of a peasant woman, Dulcinea del Toboso, whom he envisions as a princess.

On his second expedition, Don Quixote becomes more of a bandit than a savior, stealing from and hurting baffled and justifiably angry citizens while acting out against what he perceives as threats to his knighthood or to the world. Don Quixote abandons a boy, leaving him in the hands of an evil farmer simply because the farmer swears an oath that he will not harm the boy. He steals a barber's basin that he believes to be the mythic Mambrino's helmet, and he becomes convinced of the healing powers of the Balsam of Fierbras, an elixir that makes him so ill that, by comparison, he later feels healed. Sancho stands by Don Quixote, often bearing the brunt of the punishments that arise from Don Quixote's behavior.

The story of Don Quixote's deeds includes the stories of those he meets on his journey. Don Quixote witnesses the funeral of a student who dies as a result of his love for a disdainful lady turned shepherdess. He frees a wicked and devious galley slave, Gines de Pasamonte, and unwittingly reunites two bereaved couples, Cardenio and Lucinda, and Ferdinand and Dorothea. Torn apart by Ferdinand's treachery, the four lovers finally come together at an inn where Don Quixote sleeps, dreaming that he is battling a giant.

Along the way, the simple Sancho plays the straight man to Don Quixote, trying his best to correct his master's outlandish fantasies. Two of Don Quixote's friends, the priest and the barber, come to drag him home. Believing that he is under the force of an enchantment, he accompanies them, thus ending his second expedition and the First Part of the novel.

The Second Part of the novel begins with a passionate invective against a phony sequel of *Don Quixote* that was published in the interim between Cervantes's two parts. Everywhere Don Quixote goes, his reputation—gleaned by others from both the real and the false versions of the story—precedes him.

As the two embark on their journey, Sancho lies to Don Quixote, telling him that an evil enchanter has transformed Dulcinea into a peasant girl. Undoing this enchantment, in which even Sancho comes to believe, becomes Don Quixote's chief goal.

Don Quixote meets a Duke and Duchess who conspire to play tricks on him. They make a servant dress up as Merlin, for example, and tell Don Quixote that Dulcinea's enchantment—which they know to be a hoax—can be undone only if Sancho whips himself 3,300 times on his naked backside. Under the watch of the Duke and Duchess, Don Quixote and Sancho undertake several adventures. They set out on a flying wooden horse, hoping to slay a giant who has turned a princess and her lover into metal figurines and bearded the princess's female servants.

During his stay with the Duke, Sancho becomes governor of a fictitious isle. He rules for ten days until he is wounded in an onslaught the Duke and Duchess sponsor for their entertainment. Sancho reasons that it is better to be a happy laborer than a miserable governor.

A young maid at the Duchess's home falls in love with Don Quixote, but he remains a staunch worshipper of Dulcinea. Their never-consummated affair amuses the court to no end. Finally, Don Quixote sets out again on his journey, but his demise comes quickly. Shortly after his arrival in Barcelona, the Knight of the White Moon—actually an old friend in disguise—vanquishes him.

Cervantes relates the story of Don Quixote as a history, which he claims he has translated from a manuscript written by a Moor named Cide Hamete Benengeli. Cervantes becomes a party to his own fiction, even allowing Sancho and Don Quixote to modify their own histories and comment negatively upon the false history published in their names.

In the end, the beaten and battered Don Quixote forswears all the chivalric truths he followed so fervently and dies from a fever. With his death, knights-errant become extinct. Benengeli returns at the end of the novel to tell us that illustrating the demise of chivalry was his main purpose in writing the history of Don Quixote.

CHARACTER LIST

Don Quixote The novel's tragicomic hero. Don Quixote's main quest in life is to revive knight-errantry in a world devoid of chivalric virtues and values. He believes only what he chooses to believe and sees the world very differently from most people. Honest, dignified, proud, and idealistic, he wants to save the world. As intelligent as he is mad, Don Quixote starts out as an absurd and isolated figure and ends up as a pitiable and lovable old man whose strength and wisdom have failed him.

Sancho Panza The peasant laborer—greedy but kind, faithful but cowardly—whom Don Quixote takes as his squire. A representation of the common man, Sancho is a foil to Don Quixote and virtually every other character in the novel. His proverb-ridden peasant's wisdom and self-sacrificing Christian behavior prove to be the novel's most insightful and honorable worldview. He has an awestruck love for Don Quixote but grows self-confident and saucy, ending the novel by advising his master in matters of deep personal philosophy.

Rocinante Don Quixote's barn horse. Rocinante is slow but faithful, and he is as worn out as Don Quixote is.

Dapple Sancho's donkey. Dapple's disappearance and reappearance is the subject of much controversy both within the story and within the literary criticism concerning *Don Quixote*.

Cide Hamete Benengeli The fictional writer of Moorish decent from whose manuscripts Cervantes supposedly translates the novel. Cervantes uses the figure of Benengeli to comment on the ideas of authorship and literature explored in the novel and to critique historians. Benengeli's opinions, bound in his so-called historical text, show his contempt for those who write about chivalry falsely and with embellishment.

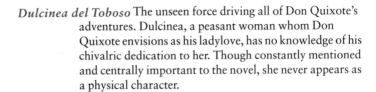

Dulcinea del Toboso The unseen force driving all of Don Quixote's adventures. Dulcinea, a peasant woman whom Don Quixote envisions as his ladylove, has no knowledge of his chivalric dedication to her. Though constantly mentioned and centrally important to the novel, she never appears as a physical character.

Cervantes The supposed translator of Benengeli's historical novel, who interjects his opinions into the novel at key times. Cervantes intentionally creates the impression that he did not invent the character of Don Quixote. Like Benengeli, Cervantes is not physically present but is a character nonetheless. In his prologues, dedications, and invention of Benengeli, Cervantes enhances the self-referential nature of the novel and forces us to think about literature's purpose and limitations.

The Duke and Duchess The cruel and haughty contrivers of the adventures that occupy Don Quixote for the majority of the novel's Second Part. Bored and snobby, the Duke and Duchess feign interest in Don Quixote and Sancho but continually play pranks on them for their personal entertainment. The Duke and Duchess spend so much money and effort on their ploys that they seem as mad as Don Quixote.

Altisidora The Duchess's bratty maid. Altisidora pretends to love Don Quixote, mocking his concept of romantic love.

Sampson Carrasco A sarcastic student from Don Quixote's village. Sampson mocks Don Quixote at first but loses to him in combat and then dedicates himself to revenge. Self-important and stuffy, Sampson fails to grasp the often playful nature of Don Quixote's madness.

The priest A friend of Don Quixote's. The priest disapproves of fictional books that, in his opinion, negatively influence society. Nonetheless, he enjoys tales of chivalry so much that he cannot throw them away. Moreover, despite his social conscience, he enjoys Don Quixote's madness at times.

The barber Don Quixote's friend who recognizes Quixote's madness but intervenes only to help the priest carry out his plans. The barber strenuously disapproves of Don Quixote's chivalry.

Teresa Panza Sancho's good-hearted wife. Teresa speaks in proverbs, exhibiting more wisdom than most other characters. Unambitious but a bit greedy, she endures Sancho's exploits and supports him with her prayers.

Cardenio An honorable man who is driven mad by the infidelities of his wife, Lucinda, and the treachery of a duke, Ferdinand. Cardenio is the quintessential romantic lover.

Lucinda Cardenio's wife. Silent and beautiful, Lucinda is a model of the courtly woman. Docile and innocent, she obliges her parents and her lover.

Ferdinand An arrogant young duke who steals Lucinda from Cardenio with no remorse.

Dorothea Ferdinand's faithful and persistent love. Dorothea flouts tradition to hunt down Ferdinand when he takes her chastity but refuses to marry her. Deceptive and cunning, smart and aggressive, Dorothea is not the typical female character of her time.

Countess Trifaldi A fictitious maidservant in distress who is impersonated by the Duke's steward. The countess's sob story sends Don Quixote and Sancho off on their expedition on the wooden horse. She is more ridiculous and fantastic than anyone except Don Quixote.

Gines de Pasamonte An ungrateful galley slave whom Don Quixote frees. Gines appears mostly for comic relief, but his justifications for his crimes force us to be more critical of Don Quixote's justifications for *his* crimes.

Roque Guinart A chivalrous bandit. Inherently conflicted, Roque believes in justice and generosity but kills an underling who challenges him for being so generous to others.

ANALYSIS OF MAJOR CHARACTERS

DON QUIXOTE DE LA MANCHA

The title character of the novel, Don Quixote is a gaunt, middle-aged gentleman who, having gone mad from reading too many books about chivalrous knights, determines to set off on a great adventure to win honor and glory in the name of his invented ladylove, Dulcinea. Don Quixote longs for a sense of purpose and beauty—two things he believes the world lacks—and hopes to bring order to a tumultuous world by reinstating the chivalric code of the knights-errant. Initially, Don Quixote's good intentions do only harm to those he meets, since he is largely unable to see the world as it really is.

As the novel progresses, Don Quixote, with the help of his faithful squire Sancho, slowly distinguishes between reality and the pictures in his head. Nonetheless, until his final sanity-inducing illness, he remains true to his chivalric conception of right and wrong. Even though his vision clears enough to reveal to him that the inns he sees are just inns, not castles as he previously believed, he never gives up on his absolute conviction that Dulcinea can save him from all misfortune. Furthermore, even when Don Quixote must retire from knight-errantry, he does so in the spirit of knight-errantry, holding to his vows and accepting his retirement as part of the terms of his defeat at the hands of the Knight of the White Moon. Despite his delusions, however, Don Quixote is fiercely intelligent and, at times, seemingly sane. He cogently and concisely talks about literature, soldiering, and government, among other topics.

No single analysis of Don Quixote's character can adequately explain the split between his madness and his sanity. He remains a puzzle throughout the novel, a character with whom we may have difficulty identifying and sympathizing. We may see Don Quixote as coy and think that he really does know what is going on around him and that he merely chooses to ignore the world and the consequences of his disastrous actions. At several times in the novel, Cervantes validates this suspicion that Don Quixote may know more than he admits. Therefore, when Don Quixote suddenly declares himself sane at the end of the novel, we wonder at his ability to shake off his madness so quickly and ask whether he has at least partly feigned this madness. On the other hand, we can read Don Quixote's character as a warning that even the most intelligent and otherwise practically minded person can fall victim to his own foolishness. Furthermore, we may see Don Quixote's adventures as a warning that chivalry—or any other outmoded set of values—can both produce positive and negative outcomes. Given the social turmoil of the period in which Cervantes wrote, this latter reading is particularly appealing. Nonetheless, all of these readings of Don Quixote's character operate in the novel.

SANCHO PANZA

The simple peasant who follows Don Quixote out of greed, curiosity, and loyalty, Sancho is the novel's only character to exist both inside and outside of Don Quixote's mad world. Other characters play along with and exploit Don Quixote's madness, but Sancho often lives in and adores it, sometimes getting caught up in the madness entirely. On the other hand, he often berates Don Quixote for his reliance on fantasy; in this sense, he is Don Quixote's foil. Whereas Don Quixote is too serious for his own good, Sancho has a quick sense of humor. Whereas Don Quixote pays lip service to a woman he has never even seen, Sancho truly loves his wife, Teresa. While Don Quixote deceives himself and others, Sancho lies only when it suits him.

Living in both Don Quixote's world and the world of his contemporaries, Sancho is able to create his own niche between them. He embodies the good and the bad aspects of both the current era and the bygone days of chivalry. He displays the faults that most of the sane characters in the novel exhibit but has an underlying honorable and compassionate streak that the others largely lack. Sancho does not share Don Quixote's maddening belief in chivalrous virtues, but he avoids swerving toward the other extreme that equates power with honor. Though Sancho begins the novel looking more like the contemporaries against whom Don Quixote rebels, he eventually relinquishes his fascination with these conventions and comes to live honorably and happily in his simple position in life. He therefore comes across as the character with the most varied perspective and the most wisdom, learning from the world around him thanks to his constant curiosity. Though Sancho is an appealing character on many levels, it is this curiosity that is responsible for much of our connection with him. He observes and thinks about Don Quixote, enabling us to judge Don Quixote. Sancho humanizes the story, bringing dignity and poise, but also humor and compassion.

Through Sancho, Cervantes critiques the ill-conceived equation of class and worth. Though Sancho is ignorant, illiterate, cowardly, and foolish, he nonetheless proves himself a wise and just ruler, a better governor the educated, wealthy, and aristocratic Duke. By the time Sancho returns home for the last time, he has gained confidence in himself and in his ability to solve problems, regardless of his lower-class status. Sancho frequently reminds his listeners that God knows what he means.

With this saying, he shows that faith in God may be a humanizing force that distinguishes truly honorable men, even when they have lower-class origins.

DULCINEA DEL TOBOSO

The unseen, unknown inspiration for all of Don Quixote's exploits, Dulcinea, we are told, is a simple peasant woman who has no knowledge of the valorous deeds that Don Quixote commits in her name. We never meet Dulcinea in the novel, and on the two occasions when it seems she might appear, some trickery keeps her away from the action. In the first case, the priest intercepts Sancho, who is on his way to deliver a letter to Dulcinea from Don Quixote. In the second instance, Sancho says that Dulcinea has been enchanted and that he thus cannot locate her.

Despite her absence from the novel, Dulcinea is an important force because she epitomizes Don Quixote's chivalric conception of the perfect woman. In his mind, she is beautiful and virtuous, and she makes up for her lack of background and lineage with her good deeds. Don Quixote describes her chiefly in poetic terms that do little to specify her qualities. She is, therefore, important not for who she is but for what her character represents and for what she indicates about Don Quixote's character.

CHARACTER ANALYSIS

THEMES, MOTIFS & SYMBOLS

THEMES

Themes are the fundamental and often universal ideas explored in a literary work.

PERSPECTIVE AND NARRATION

Don Quixote, which is composed of three different sections, is a rich exploration of the possibilities of narration. The first of these sections, comprising the chapter covering Don Quixote's first expedition, functions chiefly as a parody of contemporary romance tales. The second section, comprising the rest of the First Part, is written under the guise of a history, plodding along in historical fashion and breaking up chapters episodically, carefully documenting every day's events. The third section, which covers the Second Part of the novel, is different since it is written as a more traditional novel, organized by emotional and thematic content and filled with character development. Cervantes alone reports the story in the first section, using a straightforward narrative style. In the second section, Cervantes informs us that he is translating the manuscript of Cide Hamete Benengeli and often interrupts the narration to mention Benengeli and the internal inconsistencies in Benengeli's manuscript. Here, Cervantes uses Benengeli primarily to reinforce his claim that the story is a true history.

In the third section, however, Cervantes enters the novel as a character—as a composite of Benengeli and Cervantes the author. The characters themselves, aware of the books that have been written about them, try to alter the content of subsequent editions. This complicated and self-referential narrative structure leaves us somewhat disoriented, unable to tell which plotlines are internal to the story and which are factual. This disorientation engrosses us directly in the story and emphasizes the question of sanity that arises throughout the novel. If someone as mad as Don Quixote can write his own story, we wonder what would prevent us from doing the same. Cervantes gives us many reasons to doubt him in the second section. In the third section, however, when we are aware of another allegedly false version of the novel and a second Don Quixote, we lose all our footing and have no choice but to abandon ourselves to the story and trust Cervantes. However, having already given us reasons to distrust him, Cervantes forces us to question fundamental principles of narration, just as Quixote forces his contemporaries to question their lifestyles and principles. In this way, the form of the novel mirrors its function, creating a universe in which Cervantes entertains and instructs us, manipulating our preconceptions to force us to examine them more closely.

INCOMPATIBLE SYSTEMS OF MORALITY

Don Quixote tries to be a flesh-and-blood example of a knight-errant in an attempt to force his contemporaries to face their own failure to maintain the old system of morality, the chivalric code. This conflict between the old and the new reaches an absolute impasse: no one understands Don Quixote, and he understands no one. Only the simple-minded Sancho, with both self-motivated desires and a basic understanding of morality, can mediate between Don Quixote and the rest of the world. Sancho often subscribes to the morals of his day but then surprises us by demonstrating a belief in the anachronistic morals of chivalry as well.

In the First Part of the novel, we see the impasse between Don Quixote and those around him. Don Quixote cannot, for instance, identify with the priest's rational perspective and objectives, and Don Quixote's belief in enchantment appears ridiculous to the priest. Toward the end of the Second Part, however, Cervantes compromises between these two seemingly incompatible systems of morality, allowing Don Quixote's imaginary world and the commonplace world of the Duke and the Duchess to infiltrate each other. As the two worlds begin to mix, we start to see the advantages and disadvantages of each. Sancho ultimately prevails, subscribing to his timeless aphorisms and ascetic discipline on the one hand and using his rational abilities to adapt to the present on the other.

THE DISTINCTION BETWEEN CLASS AND WORTH

Distinguishing between a person's class and a person's worth was a fairly radical idea in Cervantes's time. In *Don Quixote,* Cervantes attacks the conventional notion that aristocrats are automatically respectable and noble. The contrast between the Duke and Duchess's thoughtless malice and Sancho's anxiety-ridden compassion highlights this problem of class. Despite his low social status, the peasant Sancho is wise and thoughtful. Likewise, the lowly goatherds and shepherds often appear as philosophers. In contrast, the cosmopolitan or aristocratic characters like the Duke and Duchess are often frivolous and unkind. Cervantes's emphasis on these disparities between class and worth is a primary reason that *Don Quixote* was such a revolutionary work in its time.

MOTIFS

Motifs are recurring structures, contrasts, or literary devices that can help to develop and inform the text's major themes.

HONOR

Some characters in *Don Quixote* show a deep concern for their personal honor and some do not. Cervantes implies that either option can lead to good or disastrous results. Anselmo, for example, is so overly protective of his wife's honor that he distrusts her fidelity, which ultimately results in her adultery and his death. Likewise, Don Quixote's obsession with his honor leads him to do battle with parties who never mean him offense or harm. On the other hand, Dorothea's concern for her personal honor leads her to pursue Ferdinand, with happy results for both of them. In these examples, we see that characters who are primarily concerned with socially prescribed codes of honor, such as Anselmo and Don Quixote, meet with difficulty, while those who set out merely to protect their own personal honor, such as Dorothea, meet with success.

Other characters, especially those who exploit Don Quixote's madness for their own entertainment, seem to care very little about their personal honor. The Duke and Duchess show that one's true personal honor has nothing to do with the honor typically associated with one's social position. Fascination with such public conceptions of honor can be taken to an extreme, dominating one's life and leading to ruin. Sancho initially exhibits such a fascination, confusing honor with social status, but he eventually comes to the realization that excessive ambition only creates trouble. In this sense, Cervantes implies that personal honor can be a powerful and positive motivating force while socially prescribed notions of honor, which are often hollow and false, can be destructive if adhered to obsessively.

ROMANCE

Though many people in Don Quixote's world seem to have given up on romantic love, Don Quixote and a few other characters hold dear this ideal. Don Louis's love for Clara, Camacho's wedding, and the tale of the captive and Zoraida, for instance, are all situations in which romantic love rises above all else. Even in the case of Sancho and Teresa, romantic love prevails as a significant part of matrimonial commitment, which we see in Teresa's desire to honor her husband at court. Ironically, Don Quixote's own devotion to Dulcinea mocks romantic love, pushing it to the extreme as he idolizes a woman he has never even seen.

LITERATURE

Don Quixote contains several discussions about the relative merits of different types of literature, including fiction and historical literature. Most of the characters, including the priest and the canon of Toledo, ultimately maintain that literature should tell the truth. Several even propose that the government should practice censorship to prevent the evil falsehoods of certain books from corrupting innocent minds like Don Quixote's. However, we see that even the true histories in the novel end up disclosing falsehoods. Cervantes declares that *Don Quixote* itself is not fiction but a translation of a historical account. The fact that we know that this claim of Cervantes's is false—since the work is fictional—makes Cervantes's symbolism clear: no matter how truthful a writer's intentions may be, he or she can never tell the whole truth. Despite these inherent flaws, however, literature remains a powerful force in the novel, guiding the lives of many characters, especially Don Quixote. Notions of authorship and storytelling preoccupy the characters throughout the novel, since many of them consider the idea of writing their own histories as their own narrators.

SYMBOLS

Symbols are objects, characters, figures, or colors used to represent abstract ideas or concepts.

BOOKS AND MANUSCRIPTS

The books and manuscripts that appear everywhere in *Don Quixote* symbolize the importance and influence of fiction and literature in everyday life. The books instruct and inform the ignorant and provide an imaginative outlet for characters with otherwise dull lives.

HORSES

Horses symbolize movement and status in the novel and often denote a character's worth or class. The pilgrims outside Barcelona, for instance, walk to the city. The noblemen ride in carriages, and the robbers and Don Quixote ride on horseback. In Don Quixote's mind, at least, the appearance of horses on the horizon symbolizes the coming of a new adventure. Indeed, Rocinante and Dapple play an important role in the journeys of Don Quixote and Sancho; they are not only means of transport and symbols of status but also companions.

INNS

The inns that appear throughout the novel are meeting places for people of all classes. They are the only locations in the novel where ordinarily segregated individuals speak and exchange stories. Inns symbolize rest and food but also corruption and greed, since many innkeepers in the novel are devious. Sancho often longs to stay at an inn rather than follow Don Quixote's chivalric desire to sleep under the stars. These opposing preferences show Sancho's connection with reality and society and his instinctive desire for comfort, in contrast to Don Quixote's alienation from society and its norms. Even when he does stay at inns, Don Quixote is noticeably alienated from the major events that take place there, such as the reunification of the four lovers in the First Part.

Summary & Analysis

The First Part, The Author's Dedication of the First Part– Chapter IV

The Author's Dedication of the First Part
Cervantes respectfully dedicates his novel to the Duke of Bejar and asks him to protect the novel from ignorant and unjust criticism.

Prologue
Cervantes belittles his novel and denies that Don Quixote is an invented character, claiming that he, Cervantes, is merely rewriting history. He reports a likely fictional account of a conversation with a friend who reassures Cervantes that his novel can stand without conventional embellishments, such as sonnets, ballads, references to famous authors, and Latin phrases. He humorously suggests that such adornments can be added to a book after its completion. Cervantes accepts this advice and urges us to enjoy the novel for its simplicity.

Chapter I
Cervantes mentions an eccentric gentleman from an unnamed village in La Mancha. The man has neglected his estate, squandered his fortune, and driven himself mad by reading too many books about chivalry. Now gaunt at fifty, the gentleman decides to become a knight-errant and set off on a great adventure in pursuit of eternal glory. He polishes his old family armor and makes a new pasteboard visor for his helmet. He finds an old nag, which he renames Rocinante, and takes the new name Don Quixote de la Mancha. Deciding he needs a lady in whose name to perform great deeds, he renames a farm girl on whom he once had a crush, Dulcinea del Toboso.

Chapter II
Don Quixote sets off on his first adventure, the details of which Cervantes claims to have discovered in La Mancha's archives. After a day-long ride, Don Quixote stops at an inn for supper and repose. He mistakes the scheming innkeeper for the keeper of a castle and mistakes two prostitutes he meets outside for princesses. He recites poetry to the two prostitutes, who laugh at him but play along. They remove his armor and feed him dinner. He refuses to remove his helmet, which is stuck on his head, but he enjoys his meal because he believes he is in a great castle where princesses are entertaining him.

CHAPTER III

In the middle of dinner, Don Quixote realizes that he has not been properly knighted. He begs the innkeeper to do him the honor. The innkeeper notes Don Quixote's madness but agrees to his request for the sake of sport, addressing him in flowery language. He tries to cheat Don Quixote, but Don Quixote does not have any money. The innkeeper commands him always to carry some in the future.

Trouble arises when guests at the inn try to use the inn's well, where Don Quixote's armor now rests, to water their animals. Don Quixote, riled and invoking Dulcinea's name, knocks one guest unconscious and smashes the skull of another. Alarmed, the innkeeper quickly performs a bizarre knighting ceremony and sends Don Quixote on his way. Don Quixote begs the favor of the two prostitutes, thanks the innkeeper for knighting him, and leaves.

CHAPTER IV

On the way home to fetch money and fresh clothing, Don Quixote hears crying and finds a farmer whipping a young boy. The farmer explains that the boy has been failing in his duties; the boy complains that his master has not been paying him. Don Quixote, calling the farmer a knight, tells him to pay the boy. The boy tells Don Quixote that the farmer is not a knight, but Don Quixote ignores him. The farmer swears by his knighthood that he will pay the boy. As Don Quixote rides away, satisfied, the farmer flogs the boy even more severely.

Don Quixote then meets a group of merchants and orders them to proclaim the beauty of Dulcinea. The merchants inadvertently insult her, and Don Quixote attacks them. But Rocinante stumbles in mid-charge, and Don Quixote falls pitifully to the ground. One of the merchants' mule-drivers beats Don Quixote and breaks his lance. The group departs, leaving Don Quixote face down near the road.

ANALYSIS: DEDICATION–CHAPTER IV

Cervantes's declaration that Don Quixote is not his own invention layers the novel with self-deception. Claiming to be recounting a history he has uncovered, Cervantes himself becomes a character in the tale. He is a kind of scholar, leading us through the story and occasionally interrupting to clarify points. But Cervantes's claim to be historically accurate does not always ring true—he does not, for example, name Don Quixote's town. Instead, he draws attention to his decision *not* to name the town by saying he does "not wish to name" this "certain village" where Don Quixote lives. In this manner, Cervantes undermines his assertion that *Don Quixote* is historical. Ironically, every time he interrupts the novel's story to remind us that it is historical fact rather than fiction, he is reminding us that the story is indeed fiction. We thus become skeptical about Cervantes's claims and begin to read his interruptions as tongue-in-cheek. In this way, the content of the novel mirrors its form: both Don Quixote and Cervantes deceive themselves.

On its surface, *Don Quixote* is a parody of chivalric tales. Cervantes mocks his hero constantly: Don Quixote's first adventure brings failure, not the rewards of a successful and heroic quest, such as treasure, glory, or a beautiful woman. But to Don Quixote, the adventure is not a complete disaster—the prostitutes receive honors, and he becomes a knight. His unwavering belief in his quest fills the tale with a romantic sense of adventure akin to that in other tales of chivalry. Thus, as much as Cervantes scorns the genre of romantic literature, he embraces it to some degree. Furthermore, though he claims in the prologue not to need sonnets, ballads, great authors, or Latin, he peppers the text with all of these conventions. In this way, the novel both parodies and emulates tales of chivalry.

Other characters' reactions to Don Quixote highlight his tragic role. Unlike us, these characters do not see that Don Quixote is motivated by good intentions, and to them he appears bizarre and dangerous. The innkeeper, who throws Don Quixote out after he attacks the other guests, typifies many characters' fears. But some characters are genuinely charmed by Don Quixote's yearnings for the simplicity of a bygone era. The two prostitutes do not understand Don Quixote's poetry, but he wins them over with his adamant belief in their royal status. On the one hand, his attempts at chivalry open others' eyes to a world for which they inwardly pine. On the other hand, his clumsiness makes his entire project seem utterly foolish. From our perspective, he is not just absurd but tragic. Though he wishes for the best, he often brings about the worst, as in the case of the young boy whom he inadvertently harms because he cannot see that the boy's master is lying. In this way, Don Quixote's complex character at once endears him to us and repulses us, since we see that his fantasies and good intentions sometimes bring pain to others.

CHAPTERS V–X

CHAPTER V

A laborer finds Don Quixote lying near the road and leads him home on his mule. Don Quixote showers the laborer with chivalric verse, comparing his troubles to those of the great knights about whom he has read. The laborer waits for night before entering the town with Don Quixote, in hopes of preserving the wounded man's dignity. But Don Quixote's friends the barber and the priest are at his house. They have just resolved to investigate his books when Don Quixote and the laborer arrive. The family receives Don Quixote, feeds him, and sends him to bed.

Chapter VI

The priest and the barber begin an inquisition into Don Quixote's library to burn the books of chivalry. Though the housekeeper wants merely to exorcise any spirits with holy water, Don Quixote's niece prefers to burn all the books. Over the niece's and the housekeeper's objections, the priest insists on reading each book's title before condemning it. He knows many of the stories and saves several of the books due to their rarity or style. He suggests that all the poetry be saved but decides against it because the niece fears that Don Quixote will then become a poet—a vocation even worse than knight-errant.

The priest soon discovers a book by Cervantes, who he claims is a friend of his. He says that Cervantes's work has clever ideas but that it never fulfills its potential. He decides to keep the novel, expecting that the sequel Cervantes has promised will eventually be published.

Chapter VII

Don Quixote wakes, still delusional, and interrupts the priest and the barber. Having walled up the entrance to the library, they decide to tell Don Quixote that an enchanter has carried off all his books and the library itself. That night, the housekeeper burns all the books. Two days later, when Don Quixote rises from bed and looks for his books, his niece tells him that an enchanter came on a cloud with a dragon, took the books due to a grudge he held against Don Quixote, and left the house full of smoke. Don Quixote believes her and explains that he recognizes this enchanter as his archrival, who knows that Don Quixote will defeat the enchanter's favorite knight.

Don Quixote's niece begs him to abandon his quest, but he refuses. He promises an illiterate laborer, Sancho Panza, that he will make him governor of an isle if Sancho leaves his wife, Teresa, and children to become Don Quixote's squire. Sancho agrees, and after he acquires a donkey, they ride from the village, discussing the isle.

Chapter VIII

After a full day, Don Quixote and Sancho come to a field of windmills, which Don Quixote mistakes for giants. Don Quixote charges at one at full speed, and his lance gets caught in the windmill's sail, throwing him and Rocinante to the ground. Don Quixote assures Sancho that the same enemy enchanter who has stolen his library turned the giants into windmills at the last minute.

The two ride on, and Don Quixote explains to Sancho that knights-errant should never complain of injury or hunger. He tears a branch from a tree to replace the lance he broke in the windmill encounter. He and Sancho camp for the night, but Don Quixote does not sleep and instead stays up all night remembering his love, Dulcinea.

SUMMARY & ANALYSIS

The next day, Don Quixote and Sancho encounter two monks and a carriage carrying a lady and her attendants. Don Quixote thinks that the two monks are enchanters who have captured a princess and attacks them, ignoring Sancho's and the monks' protests. He knocks one monk off his mule. Sancho, believing he is rightly taking spoils from Don Quixote's battle, begins to rob the monk of his clothes. The monks' servants beat Sancho, and the two monks ride off.

Don Quixote tells the lady to return to Toboso and present herself to Dulcinea. He argues with one of her attendants and soon gets into a battle with him. Cervantes describes the battle in great detail but cuts off the narration just as Don Quixote is about to deliver the mortal blow. Cervantes explains that the historical account from which he has been working ends at precisely this point.

CHAPTER IX

Cervantes says he was quite irked by this break in the text, believing that such a knight deserves to have his tale told by a great sage. He says that he was at a fair in the Spanish city of Toledo when he discovered a boy selling Arabic parchments in the street. He hired a Moor to read him some of the stories. When the Moor began to translate one line about Dulcinea, which read that she was "the best hand at salting pork of any woman in all La Mancha," Cervantes rushed the Moor to his home to have him translate the whole parchment.

According to Cervantes, the parchment contained the history of Don Quixote, written by Cide Hamete Benengeli. From this point on, Cervantes claims, his work is a translation of Benengeli's story. This second portion of the manuscript begins with the conclusion of the preceding chapter's battle. The attendant gives Don Quixote a mighty blow, splitting his ear. Don Quixote knocks the man down and threatens to kill him. He spares him when several ladies traveling with the man promise that the man will present himself to Dulcinea.

CHAPTER X

Afterward, Sancho begs Don Quixote to make him governor of the isle that he believes they have won in battle. Don Quixote assures him that he will fulfill his promise soon. Sancho then begins to worry that the authorities might come after them for beating the lady's attendant. Don Quixote assures Sancho that knights never go to jail, since they are permitted to use violence in the pursuit of justice.

Sancho offers to care for Don Quixote's bleeding ear. Don Quixote tells him about the Balsam of Fierbras, which he says has the power to cure any wound and is easy to make. Sancho suggests that they could make money by producing the balsam, but Don Quixote dismisses the suggestion. Upon seeing the damage the attendant did to his helmet, he swears revenge, but Sancho reminds him that the attendant promised to present himself to Dulcinea in return. Don Quixote abandons his oath of revenge and swears to maintain a strict lifestyle until he gets a new helmet. Unable to secure other lodging, the two sleep out under the sky, which pleases Don Quixote's romantic sensibilities but displeases Sancho.

ANALYSIS: CHAPTERS V–X

In every way Don Quixote's opposite, Sancho Panza serves as a simple-minded foil to his master's complex madness. Cervantes contrasts these two men even on the most fundamental levels: Don Quixote is tall and gaunt and deprives himself in his pursuit of noble ideals, while Sancho is short and pudgy and finds happiness in the basic pleasures of food and wine. Sancho is a peace-loving laborer who leaves his family only after Don Quixote promises to make him a governor. Don Quixote's violent idealism befuddles Sancho, who consistently warns his master about the error of his ways. Sancho eats when he is hungry but accepts Don Quixote's fasting as a knightly duty. He complains when he is hurt and marvels at his master's capacity to withstand suffering. Sancho's perception of Don Quixote informs our own perception of him, and we identify and sympathize with the bumbling Sancho because he reacts to Don Quixote the way most people would. Through Sancho, we see Don Quixote as a human being with an oddly admirable yet challenging outlook on life.

At the same time, Sancho makes it difficult to sympathize with him since he participates in his master's fantasy world when it suits his own interests. In robbing the monk, for instance, Sancho pretends to believe that he is claiming the spoils of war. He takes advantage of Don Quixote's sincere belief in a fantasy world to indulge his greed, a trait that does not fit with our conception of Sancho as an innocent peasant.

Unlike many of the novel's battle scenes, which at times seem mechanical and plodding, the battle between Don Quixote and the attendant is genuinely suspenseful. As opposed to the fight scene with the guests at the inn or the charge at the windmills, this battle is graphic. Unlike Don Quixote's previous foes—inanimate objects, unsuspecting passersby, or disapproving brutes—the attendant attacks Don Quixote with genuine zeal, which, along with the attendant's skill, heightens the battle's suspense. The attendant accepts the myth Don Quixote presents him—that they are two great enemies battling for honor. The fight thus takes on epic proportions for Don Quixote, and its form underscores these proportions, since the men verbally spar, choose their weapons, and engage. After several blows, the battle concludes when Don Quixote defeats his opponent and forces him to submit to the humiliaton of presenting himself to Dulcinea.

Cervantes's sudden interruption of the narrative draws attention to the deficiencies of the work and, by implication, those of other heroic tales. Cervantes's claim that the tale is factual is undercut when he stops the story due to a gap in the alleged historial account. Cervantes seems to be showing his scholarship by cutting off the narrative to credit its source, but the source he then describes turns out to be incomplete. At best, *Don Quixote* now appears to be a translation—and not even Cervantes's own translation—which gives the novel a more mythical feel. Though myths are powerful for those who believe them, they are vulnerable to distortion with each storyteller's version. In forcing us to question the validity of the story during one of its most dramatic moments, Cervantes implicitly criticizes the authorship and authenticity of all heroic tales.

In his famous charge at the windmills, we see that Don Quixote persists in living in a fantasy world even when he is able to see reality for a moment. Don Quixote briefly connects with reality after Sancho points out that the giants are merely windmills, but Don Quixote immediately makes an excuse, claiming that the enchanter has deceived him. This enchanter is not entirely fictional—Don Quixote has so deceived himself with his books of chivalry that he seeks to make up excuses even in the face of reality. Throughout the novel, Cervantes analyzes the dangers inherent in the overzealous pursuit of ideals, as we see Don Quixote continually constructing stories to explain a belief system that is often at odds with reality.

THE FIRST PART, CHAPTERS XI–XV

CHAPTER XI

Don Quixote and Sancho join a group of goatherds for the night. They eat and drink together, and Sancho gets drunk on the goatherds' wine while Don Quixote tells the group about the "golden age" in which virgins roamed the world freely and without fear. He says that knights were created to protect the purity of these virgins. A singing goatherd then arrives. At the request of the others and despite Sancho's protests, he sings a love ballad to the group. One of the goatherds dresses Don Quixote's wounded ear with a poultice that heals it.

CHAPTER XII

A goatherd named Peter arrives with news that the shepherd-student Chrysostom has died from his love for Marcela. As Peter tells the story of the lovesick Chrysostom, Don Quixote interrupts several times to correct Peter's poor speech. Peter explains that Marcela is a wealthy, beautiful orphan who has abandoned her wealth for a shepherdess's life. Modest and kind, Marcela charms everyone but refuses to marry, which has given her a reputation for cruelty in affairs of the heart. The goatherds invite Don Quixote to accompany them to Chrysostom's burial the next day, and he accepts. They all go to sleep except for Don Quixote, who stays up all night sighing for Dulcinea.

CHAPTER XIII

On the way to the funeral, a traveler named Vivaldo asks Don Quixote why he wears armor in such a peaceful country. Don Quixote explains the principles of knighthood. Vivaldo compares the severity of the knight's lifestyle to that of a monk's, and Don Quixote says that knights execute the will of God for which the monks pray.

Vivaldo and Don Quixote discuss knight-errantry, and Don Quixote explains that tradition dictates that knights-errant dedicate themselves to ladies rather than to God. He adds that all knights-errant are in love, even if they do not show it. He describes Dulcinea to the company in flowery and poetic terms. The group then arrives at the burial site, where six men carrying Chrysostom's body arrive. Chrysostom's friend Ambrosio makes a speech exalting the deceased, and Vivaldo asks him to save some of Chrysostom's poetry despite Chrysostom's request that it be burned. Vivaldo takes one poem, and Ambrosio asks him to read it aloud.

CHAPTER XIV

Vivaldo reads the poem aloud. It praises Marcela's beauty, laments her cruelty, and ends with Chrysostom's dying wish that famous Greek mythical characters receive him in the afterlife. Marcela herself then appears and claims never to have given Chrysostom or any of her other suitors any hope of winning her affection. She attributes all her beauty to heaven and says she is not at fault for remaining chaste. Marcela leaves before Ambrosio can respond. Some of the men try to follow her, but Don Quixote says he will kill anyone who pursues her. He then follows Marcela to offer her his services.

CHAPTER XV

Don Quixote and Sancho stop to rest and eat lunch. Rocinante wanders off into a herd of mares owned by a group of Yanguesans and tries to mate with them. The Yanguesans beat Rocinante. Don Quixote then attacks the numerous Yanguesans, and he and Sancho lose the battle. While lying on the ground, Don Quixote and Sancho discuss the balsam that, Don Quixote claims, knights use to cure wounds. Don Quixote blames their defeat on the fact that he drew his sword against non-knights, a clear violation of the chivalric code. The two quarrel about the value that fighting has in the life of a knight-errant. On Don Quixote's orders, Sancho leads him to an inn on his donkey. They arrive at another inn, which Don Quixote mistakes for a castle.

ANALYSIS: CHAPTERS XI–XV

Peter portrays Marcela as unduly arrogant, and we suspect that her obsessions, like Don Quixote's, may cause others to suffer. But when we meet Marcela, we find that she is intelligent and defends herself articulately, reasoning that if men suffer for her beauty, it is their fault. Chrysostom, not Marcela, turns out to be the fool, falling so deeply in love with his romantic ideal that he kills himself. This outcome adds to Cervantes's ongoing critique of those who are obsessed with outdated notions of chivalry. Though Marcela may have abandoned certain customs of the day, she is not a fool. She is an example of someone who ignores outdated customs in an intelligent way.

The story of Marcela and Chrysostom, which has its own characters and moral lesson, marks a change in the structure of the novel, as Don Quixote is a mere observer rather than a participant. Here, Cervantes begins to focus on the social setting in which Don Quixote operates. The goatherds, for instance, represent a new class of characters, that of pastoral people living off the earth. Unlike those we meet earlier, such as the innkeeper, the prostitutes, and the farm boy and his master, the characters we meet in this section are important not merely for their reactions to Don Quixote, but as fully developed characters in their own right.

Peter's narration of the story about Marcela and Chrysostom is a subtle criticism of the tradition of oral storytelling. We hear about Marcela first from Peter and later from Ambrosio and from Chrysostom's poem. The difference between her character in the story and her character in reality highlights a problem Cervantes explores throughout the novel: not all stories are true, and in this particular case, the more a story is repeated and passed on, the more it diverges from the truth. This criticism, of course, can be applied to Cervantes's novel itself, as well as to the chivalric tales that have driven Don Quixote mad.

THE FIRST PART, CHAPTERS XVI–XX

CHAPTER XVI

Rather than admit that Don Quixote received a vicious thrashing from a gang of Yanguesans, Sancho tells the innkeeper that his master fell and injured himself. The innkeeper's wife and beautiful daughter tend to Don Quixote's wounds. Don Quixote begins to believe that the daughter has fallen in love with him and that she has promised to lie with him that night. In actuality, Maritornes, the daughter's hunchbacked servant, creeps in that night to sleep with a carrier who is sharing a room with Don Quixote and Sancho. As an aside, Cervantes then tells us that Cide Hamete Benengeli specially mentions the carrier because Benengeli is related to him.

Nearly blind, Maritornes accidentally goes to Don Quixote's bed instead of the carrier's. Don Quixote mistakes her for the beautiful daughter and tries to woo her, and the carrier attacks him. Maritornes jumps into Sancho's bed to hide. Awakened by the commotion, the innkeeper goes to the bedroom and he, the carrier, and Sancho have a terrific brawl. An officer staying at the inn hears the fighting and goes upstairs to break it up. The officer sees Don Quixote passed out on the bed and believes he is dead. He leaves to get a light to investigate the scene.

CHAPTER XVII

Don Quixote tells Sancho that the inn is enchanted and recounts his version of the evening's events. He says a princess came in to woo him and a giant beat him up. Just then, the officer returns, and Don Quixote insults him, provoking him to beat Don Quixote. Sancho, angry about his own injuries, rails against Don Quixote's story, but Don Quixote promises to make the balsam to cure Sancho. He tells Sancho not to get angry over enchantments, since they cannot be stopped.

Don Quixote mixes ingredients and drinks the potion. He vomits immediately and passes out. Upon waking, he feels much better and believes he has successfully concocted the mythical balsam. Sancho also takes the potion, and although it makes him tremendously ill, he does not vomit. Don Quixote explains that the balsam does not work on Sancho because he is a squire and not a knight.

As Don Quixote leaves the inn, the innkeeper demands that he pay for his stay. Surprised that he has stayed in an inn and not a castle, Don Quixote refuses to pay on the grounds that knights-errant never pay for lodging. He rides off, slinging insults at the innkeeper. Several rogues at the inn capture Sancho, who also refuses to pay, and toss him in a blanket. Don Quixote, too bruised to dismount from Rocinante, believes that the enchantment prevents him from helping Sancho. Sancho finally gets away and feels proud for not having paid. But it turns out that the innkeeper has stolen Sancho's saddlebags.

CHAPTER XVIII

As they ride away from the inn, Sancho complains bitterly to Don Quixote about the injuries their misadventures cause him. Suddenly Don Quixote sees clouds of dust coming along the road and mistakes them for two great armies on the brink of battle. Sancho warns his master that the two clouds actually come from two herds of sheep. Unconvinced, Don Quixote describes in great detail the knights he thinks he sees in the dust. Cervantes eventually cuts off the account, remarking that Don Quixote is merely reeling off ideas he has encountered in his "lying books" about chivalry.

Don Quixote rushes into the battle and kills seven sheep before two shepherds throw stones at him and knock out several of his teeth. San-

cho points out that the armies were really just sheep, prompting Don
Quixote to explain that a sorcerer turned the armies into sheep in the
midst of battle to thwart his efforts. Don Quixote takes more of the balsam, and as Sancho comes close to see how badly his master's teeth have
been injured, Don Quixote vomits on him. Nauseous, Sancho then
vomits on Don Quixote. When Sancho tries to fetch something to clean
them up, he discovers that his saddlebags have been stolen. Fed up, he
vows to go home. Don Quixote says that he would rather sleep in an inn
that night than in the field, and tells Sancho to lead them to an inn.

Chapter XIX

Sancho tells Don Quixote that their troubles stem from Don Quixote's
violation of his vow to keep a strict lifestyle until he finds a new helmet.
Don Quixote agrees, noting that he had forgotten the vow, and blames
Sancho for failing to remind him. As night falls, the two encounter a
group of priests mourning as they escort the body of a dead man. When
the priests refuse to identify themselves, Don Quixote knocks one of
them off his horse, and the others scatter. Don Quixote tells the
wounded priest that he has come to avenge injuries. The priest complains that Don Quixote has injured him without avenging anything.

Sancho steals goods from the priest's mule. As the priest rides away,
Sancho yells after him that this mischief was the work of Don Quixote,
the Knight of the Sad Countenance. Pleased with his new title, Don
Quixote asks Sancho where he came up with it. Sancho replies that Don
Quixote's face looks sad without its teeth. But Don Quixote asserts that
Sancho so named him because a sage, who Don Quixote claims is dic-
tating his life's story, made Sancho think of this title. The two ride into
a valley and eat dinner. They then have a conversation that Cervantes
promises to record in the next chapter.

Chapter XX

Don Quixote and Sancho hear a scary pounding. Sancho implores his
master to wait until morning to investigate the sound, but Don Quixote
swears to take on the unknown foe. Don Quixote tells Sancho to wait
three days and then report his death to Dulcinea if he has not returned.
Sancho secretly ties up Rocinante's legs, immobilizing him, and Don
Quixote concedes that since Rocinante seems unable to move, he must
wait until morning to investigate.

Sancho begins telling a story. He tells each detail twice, and Don
Quixote interrupts and commands him to tell the story only once. But
Sancho says that this is the way stories are told in his homeland, so Don
Quixote allows him to proceed. Sancho then vividly describes a shepherdess. Don Quixote asks whether he knew the shepherdess. Sancho
says that he did not but that when he first heard the story it seemed so
real that he could swear he had seen her. Sancho tells how a shepherd in

love with this shepherdess had to cross a river with a herd of goats, and Sancho instructs Don Quixote to keep count while he tells the story of how many goats the character takes across. Midway through, Don Quixote tells Sancho to proceed with the story as though all the goats were already across. Sancho asks his master whether he knows how many goats have already crossed, and Don Quixote admits that he does not. Sancho ends his story, and Don Quixote cannot persuade him to tell the rest of it.

In the morning, Sancho and Don Quixote set off. Cervantes says that Sancho's faithfulness convinces Don Quixote that Sancho is a good man. When the two arrive at a small bunch of houses by a river, they discover that the scary pounding comes from fulling-hammers, which are used to beat cloth. Sancho laughs, and Don Quixote hits him with his lance. Don Quixote says that Sancho must speak less to him in the future. Sancho accepts the order after Don Quixote tells him that he has left Sancho money in his will.

ANALYSIS: CHAPTERS XVI–XX

The graphic accounts of Don Quixote's and Sancho's vomiting constitute Cervantes's basest humor. Cervantes later justifies the inclusion of such bawdy episodes, stating that a successful novel contains elements that appeal to all levels of society. This crude humor seems out of place, especially when compared to the delicate humor of Sancho's story in Chapter XX. Critics often focus on this disparity, but Cervantes may be using this contrast to draw our attention to the differences between romantic ideals and reality. He highlights reality by emphasizing its physical aspects, reminding us about the inconsistency between the way things play out in Don Quixote's dreams and the way they play out in the real world.

Don Quixote's explanation for why the Balsam of Fierbras does not work for Sancho underscores the characters' perception of class and privilege. Don Quixote seems to believe that bad things cannot happen to knights because they belong to a higher class, one that the mundane world cannot touch. The fact that he persistently attributes all of his misfortunes to an enchantment emphasizes his faith that mortal forces cannot touch him. This class distinction extends to gentlemen as well, who play by a different set of rules than members of the lower class. Cervantes's attitude toward such class distinctions appears mixed: even though Cervantes includes numerous classist remarks, he pokes fun at Don Quixote's claim of being separate and superior. Ultimately, Cervantes undercuts the idea that one's class signifies one's worth. He criticizes people in all classes in an effort to humanize everyone.

Sancho's bizarre, aborted account of the shepherd and shepherdess highlights Cervantes's tendency to comment on the nature of storytelling and the way literature should be presented and read. Sancho's storytelling mimics Cardenio's later refusal, in Chapter XXIII, to finish his story when Don Quixote interrupts him in the Sierra Morena. Here, Sancho asserts his right to tell the story as he sees fit and according to the tradition by which people in his homeland tell stories. This tradition mimics great epic poems, often tedious in their apparently useless repetition and lists of detail. Don Quixote views these conventions as empty formalities and asks Sancho to skip them, which irritates Sancho. But Sancho apparently believes that a story is not truly a story unless it has a certain formal structure. This interplay of structure and content is found throughout *Don Quixote,* since Cervantes frequently plays with the highly formal framework of chivalric tales. Here, through Sancho, Cervantes implies that a reader must play along with the author's structural effects to get to the meaning of the story. Sancho's story thus prompts us to pay attention to the game Cervantes plays throughout his novel.

THE FIRST PART, CHAPTERS XXI-XXVI

> For not all those poets who praise ladies under names
> which they choose so freely, really have such mistresses.
> (See QUOTATIONS, p. 79)

CHAPTER XXI

Don Quixote and Sancho see a man on a mule with something glittering on his head. The man is a barber wearing a basin on his head to protect him from the rain. But Don Quixote mistakes the man for a great knight wearing the mythic Mambrino's helmet and vows to win the helmet from him. When the barber sees Don Quixote charging at him, the barber runs away, leaving behind his mule and basin. Sancho laughs at Don Quixote and tells him that the "helmet" is just a basin.

Don Quixote explains that the enchanted helmet must have fallen into the hands of someone who did not know its value and then melted it down, making it into a basin. He resolves to wear it in the meantime and have it made back into a helmet at the next village. When Sancho again begins to complain about the treatment he received at the inn while Don Quixote stood by idly, Don Quixote explains that Sancho's treatment was just a joke. He adds that had it been serious, he would have returned to avenge it. Don Quixote then explains how he will win the affections of a princess by fighting for her father, the king. He says he will then marry her and make Sancho rich.

CHAPTER XXII

The manuscript continues, Cervantes says, with the account of Don Quixote and Sancho's encounter with a chain gang of galley slaves. The prisoners are guarded by two armed men on foot and two armed horsemen. Sancho warns Don Quixote not to interfere with the chain gang, but Don Quixote approaches the group anyway and asks each prisoner to tell his story. Each slave makes up a story in which his criminal actions appear to be justified or even necessary. Upon seeing the men detained against their will, Don Quixote charges the officers. Anxious to be free, the prisoners join the charge. After the men gain freedom, Don Quixote commands them to present themselves to Dulcinea, which they refuse to do out of fear for their safety. Don Quixote insults them, and they attack him, running away with his and Sancho's possessions. Freeing the galley slaves distresses Sancho, who is concerned that the Holy Brotherhood, or police, will come after them. Sancho urges Don Quixote to flee into the mountains.

CHAPTER XXIII
Don Quixote and Sancho ride into the woods of the Sierra Morena. Unfortunately for them, one of the galley slaves, Gines de Pasamonte, is also hiding in these woods. Gines steals Sancho's donkey, whose name we now learn is Dapple. On the road through the mountains, Don Quixote and Sancho find a saddle and a bag containing a notebook, shirts, and money. Don Quixote gives Sancho the money, and Sancho decides that this payment makes up for all his previous troubles.

In the notebook, Don Quixote finds a poem and a love letter, which indicate that their author was spurned by his lover and driven to madness by her infidelity. Don Quixote then sees a nearly naked man hopping through the wilderness and resolves to follow him and learn his tale. Sancho opposes the idea because he wants to protect the money they have found and fears that the man might claim the money if they catch up with him. Don Quixote explains to Sancho, however, that they have no choice but to look for the naked man once they consider that the money might belong to him.

While searching for the man, Don Quixote and Sancho encounter an old goatherd who tells them the story of the naked man. A polite, rich gentleman, he appeared one day to ask the goatherds to help him locate the wildest part of the Sierra Morena. The goatherds pointed the man in a direction and he ran off. Later, he returned and assaulted one of the goatherds on the road, stealing his food. They pursued him and several days later found him in a ragged state, so they offered him food and care. The man treated them courteously at some times but rudely at others. Just as the old goatherd concludes the story, the man, whom Cervantes now calls the Ragged Knight of the Sorry Countenance, appears. Don Quixote gives him a long hug.

CHAPTER XXIV
The Ragged Knight of the Sorry Countenance asks Don Quixote for food and then says that he will tell his story as long as Don Quixote and

the others promise not to interrupt him. His name is Cardenio, and he is a wealthy nobleman from the region of Andalusia in southern Spain. From childhood he has been madly in love with the beautiful Lucinda. The two were to be married, but Cardenio received a letter from a duke requesting Cardenio's service as a companion to the Duke's son Ferdinand.

Cardenio went to the duke and met Ferdinand. Ferdinand immediately liked Cardenio and the two became friends. Ferdinand was in love with a young farmer's daughter, but he had wooed her secretly and did not want to tell his father. To avoid his father's wrath, Ferdinand decided that he needed to go away for a little while and forget about the farmer's daughter. He asked to go to Cardenio's parents' home, under the pretext of buying some horses. There, Ferdinand met Lucinda, whom he praised as one of the great beauties of the world.

Cardenio mentions that Lucinda was a fan of chivalric books. Cardenio and Don Quixote then spar over whether a queen in one of the books mentioned had an affair with her counselor. The altercation ends Cardenio's story and sends him into a fit of madness. He beats Sancho, the goatherd, and Don Quixote before running off into the wilderness.

Chapter XXV

As Sancho and Don Quixote ride away, Sancho becomes angry with his master for imposing a code of silence on him and for arguing inanely with Cardenio. Don Quixote retracts his order that Sancho remain silent but stands by his defense of the fictional queen. Don Quixote then tells Sancho that he will be staying alone in the Sierra Morena to do penance in order to win honor for himself. He says that he has been absent from Dulcinea for so long that he has concerns about her fidelity. Instead of returning to check up on her, he has decided that it would be more valorous to go mad imagining the slights his ladylove has committed against him.

Sancho derides his master's plan as folly, and Don Quixote is amazed that Sancho has not yet realized that everything knights-errant do is folly. Don Quixote writes a love letter for Sancho to convey to Dulcinea and then reveals Dulcinea's identity to him. Sancho is shocked, since he knows her to be a coarse peasant. But Don Quixote tells Sancho that many ladyloves were invented princesses whose only purpose was to inspire their knights-errant, and therefore Dulcinea is a princess if he says she is. Sancho promises to return as quickly as he can, and after watching Don Quixote take off his trousers and do a headstand to indicate his madness, he sets off on Rocinante.

Chapter XXVI

In his penance, Don Quixote decides to follow the example of the great knight Amadis, commending himself to God and praying in the name of

Dulcinea. He wanders around the valley, writing verses on trees. Sancho, on his way home, encounters the priest and the barber at the inn where he was tossed in the blanket. The priest and the barber stop him and ask him what has become of Don Quixote. Sancho tells them about his master's penance and about the letter he must deliver to Dulcinea. He explains that Don Quixote has promised to give him a governorship and a beautiful wife when Don Quixote himself becomes an emperor. The priest and the barber conclude that Sancho has gone mad and promise him in jest that Don Quixote will certainly become an emperor or at least an archbishop. This last point troubles Sancho because he fears that an archbishop would not provide him with adequate rewards. The priest and the barber then decide to go to Don Qui-xote, disguising themselves as a damsel in distress and her squire in order to trick Don Quixote into coming home again.

Analysis: Chapters XXI–XXVI

Cervantes examines the question of crime and punishment by contrasting Don Quixote's actions with the actions of the galley slaves. Like the slaves, Don Quixote believes that his criminal actions are justified. He steals the basin from the barber, but his theft seems excusable because he is a chivalrous, well-meaning madman. Though Cervantes portrays Don Quixote's crime as more excusable than the crimes of the galley slaves, we must nonetheless keep in mind that Don Quixote's actions are still crimes, regardless of the fact that he commits them in the name of chivalry. This issue arises again when a priest argues that Don Quix-ote is insane and not, therefore, liable for his behavior. Here, when Gines de Pasamonte reappears and steals Dapple to Sancho's great distress, Cervantes looks at crime from the victim's perspective. Throughout the novel, the victim's perspective—in this case Sancho's—often gets lost amid the humorous narration of Don Quixote's exploits.

Storytelling is central to *Don Quixote*. Everyone in the novel has a story, and telling these stories is a major part of the characters' lives. The abundance of stories makes the novel's narration less fluid. It is difficult to focus on Don Quixote's adventures when other characters' stories and the third-person narrator constantly interrupt us. However, these interruptions give us additional perspectives on Don Quixote's story. Cardenio's story, like the tale of Marcela and Chrysostom, does not relate directly to Don Quixote's life, but it does inspire him to action. In particular, it inspires Don Quixote's acts of penance, and this subsequent, obvious madness makes us question the heroic nature of Carde-nio's story. Though Cardenio had a valid reason for grieving, he may have, in becoming a wild man, overreacted to Lucinda's rejection, in effect choosing his madness as much as Don Quixote chooses his.

At several points in these chapters, the translator of this particular edition, J.M. Cohen, analyzes several inconsistencies in the text. In Chapter XXII, for instance, Cohen points out that the text is inconsistent on the number of guns the guards possess. In the first description, Cervantes says there are two guns, but in the battle that follows, he accounts for only one gun. In Chapter XXIII, Cohen points out that the text is inconsistent concerning Gines's theft of Dapple. Here, Gines steals Dapple, but later, Sancho is riding him through the mountains. Later, he again laments the loss of Dapple. Because Cervantes places so much emphasis throughout *Don Quixote* on the narrative layers in the story, it may be tempting to read these inconsistencies as deliberate attempts by Cervantes to remove himself even further from the narrative. It seems more likely, however, that these inconsistencies are merely unintentional errors on Cervantes's part.

THE FIRST PART, CHAPTERS XXVII–XXXI

CHAPTER XXVII

Equipped with their costumes, the priest and the barber set out with Sancho to find Don Quixote and lure him home again. Sancho relates to them the saga of his adventures as they journey. When they arrive, Sancho goes on ahead, planning to tell Don Quixote that he has seen Dulcinea, that he has given her his letter, and that she begs for Don Quixote to come home to her. If Don Quixote still refuses to come home, the priest and the barber will go ahead with their plan to pretend to be a damsel in distress who seeks his assistance.

While waiting for Sancho to return, the priest and the barber encounter Cardenio, who tells them his story, this time including the conclusion that he failed to recount to Don Quixote. Cardenio explains that Ferdinand, while visiting Cardenio's house, found a letter from Lucinda and was so taken with her that he devised a plan to win her for himself. Ferdinand sent Cardenio back to the duke's house and proposed to Lucinda. While at the duke's house, Cardenio received a letter from Lucinda begging him to come home because Ferdinand had proposed, her greedy parents had accepted, and she felt that she would soon kill herself. Cardenio rushed home just in time to see the wedding take place. Despite her words, Lucinda did not kill herself but instead accepted Ferdinand as her husband. Cardenio rushed away from the wedding and went out into the wilderness, driven mad with grief and hatred. Cervantes interrupts to say that the end of Cardenio's story marks the end of the third part of the history by Cide Hamete Benengeli.

Chapter XXVIII

Before returning to the narration, Cervantes says that Don Quixote's era is lucky that Don Quixote has brought back knight-errantry. Back in the story, the priest, the barber, and Cardenio meet a young woman named Dorothea, whom they initially take for a man because she is wearing a man's clothes. Dorothea tells her tragic story. The incredibly beautiful daughter of a wealthy farmer, she happened to attract the attention of the son of her father's master. The son wooed her persistently, but she resisted until one day when he appeared in her bedroom by trickery and swore to marry her. She succumbed to him because she was afraid he would rape her if she did not. He left town and abandoned her. Dorothea chased him in hopes of enforcing his pledge to marry her but discovered that he had already married someone else in a nearby town. She then relates the circumstances of that marriage, revealing that the son who falsely proposed to her was Ferdinand, the duke's son, and that his new bride in the nearby town was Lucinda. Dorothea tells them she then ran off into the wilderness out of shame.

Chapter XXIX

Cardenio is thrilled to learn from Dorothea that when Lucinda fainted, Ferdinand found a letter on her that revealed her love for Cardenio. Cardenio vows to help Dorothea avenge the wrong Ferdinand has done to her. Dorothea offers to play the distressed damsel in the plot to lure Don Quixote home. Sancho returns with news that Don Quixote refuses to return to Dulcinea until he has won honor through penance.

The priest tells Sancho that Dorothea is Princess Micomicona, who is seeking Don Quixote's help to redress a wrong a giant has done her. Sancho, the costumed Dorothea, and the barber, wearing a fake beard, find Don Quixote. In high poetic style, Dorothea beseeches Don Quixote to slay a giant who has taken over her kingdom. Don Quixote promises to follow her and not engage in any other adventures along the way. Sancho is pleased, believing he will now get his governorship. The priest and Cardenio overtake the party on the road. The priest greets Don Quixote, who recognizes neither the priest nor Cardenio. The priest tells Don Quixote that freed galley slaves have mugged him and the barber.

Chapter XXX

Dorothea weaves a story about the giant who has attacked her kingdom. She slips up several times during the story, even forgetting the name the priest has given her, and the priest has to interject to prevent her from revealing their ploy. Dorothea says she will marry Don Quixote after he vanquishes the giant, but Don Quixote refuses because he loves Dulcinea. His refusal upsets Sancho, who insults Dulcinea. Don Quixote beats Sancho. Just then, Gines de Pasamonte reappears with Sancho's donkey and flees on foot. Cardenio and Dorothea discuss Don

Quixote's madness, and Cardenio remarks that Don Quixote is so crazy that he is sure no author could have invented him.

CHAPTER XXXI

Don Quixote pulls Sancho aside and begs him to tell about his visit to Dulcinea. Sancho makes up a story, saying that Dulcinea was at work and did not have the time or ability to read Don Quixote's letter. As they ride along, the young boy whom Don Quixote tried to save from his master in Chapter IV appears, reviling Don Quixote for stupidly accepting his master's word and leaving him to a worse beating. Don Quixote swears that he will reap vengeance on the young shepherd's master, but the young shepherd tells Don Quixote not to interfere in the future, fearing that he would only make matters worse.

ANALYSIS: XVII–XXXI

Don Quixote's madness begins to impose itself on other characters with the scheme the priest concocts to lure Don Quixote home. Though Don Quixote's madness is his own invention, his refusal to break out of it forces the others to participate in it if they wish to engage him. This madness and play-acting intensifies in these chapters, especially when everyone in the company is forced to adhere to Dorothea's story to prevent the trickery from being revealed. The group's constant playacting makes the fictional details of their stories into imitations of reality and makes reality an imitatation of their stories. Dorothea's story about the giant, for instance, closely resembles her own plight: the real-life Ferdinand has run off with her virginity just as the fictional giant has supposedly run off with her kingdom. Dorothea is, in fact, quite similar to the princess-in-exile she pretends to be in the trick: like the character she plays, she cannot return home out of shame.

Amid this blurring between fiction and reality, Sancho's character stands out as the mediator between madness and sanity. Unlike the others, each of whom is either entirely mad or entirely sane, Sancho straddles the line between the real world and the fictional world. He sometimes sees the truth, but sometimes falls for trickery. Seemingly half-conscious of what is going on around him, Sancho can be deceived into believing that Dorothea is really a princess but can just as easily deceive Don Quixote into believing that he has gone to see Dulcinea. Sancho's perspective proves important in the novel because through him we can judge Don Quixote's madness more fairly. We recognize the complexity of Don Quixote's madness when we see Sancho get carried away by it even when he seems to recognize it for what it is.

Ironically, Dorothea makes mistakes in her fictional story in the same chapter in which Dapple reappears even though he is supposedly already present. Cohen and others conclude that this inconsistency concerning Dapple indicates nothing more than an oversight on the part of Cervantes, a failure to edit the text fully before sending it to publication. Cohen suggests that if the error were unintentional, it might indicate that Cervantes intended the story be told orally, and so such small details would be more likely to pass unnoticed. But one can argue that if the error was unintentional, Cervantes tried to make it seem intentional when he published the second half of the novel a decade later. At the beginning of the Second Part, the characters actually discuss the First Part and conclude that its inconsistencies concerning Dapple can be corrected in a second printing of novels. This discussion highlights the fictitious nature of the novel, fitting in with the idea that literature is unable to tell the whole truth.

THE FIRST PART, CHAPTERS XXXII–XXXVII

CHAPTER XXXII

> *I shall never be fool enough to turn knight-errant. For I see quite well that it's not the fashion now to do as they did in the olden days when they say those famous knights roamed the world.* (See QUOTATIONS, p. 79)

Don Quixote, Sancho, the priest, the barber, Dorothea, and Cardenio arrive at the same inn where Sancho was tossed in the blanket. The barber takes off his disguise. The innkeeper, his wife, their daughter, and Maritornes join the priest, the barber, Dorothea, and Cardenio to talk about Don Quixote's madness and the books that have caused it. The priest and the barber want to burn the inn's collection of chivalric literature, but the innkeeper defends these tales, claiming that the government would not allow them to be published if they were untrue. But he adds that he will never become a knight-errant, because he knows chivalry is out of style. He tells the company that an unnamed man left an old trunk filled with books and manuscripts at the inn. The priest, despite his skepticism about the books of chivalry, asks the innkeeper for permission to copy one of the manuscripts, which the priest reads to the crowd.

CHAPTER XXXIII

The manuscript that the priest reads tells the story of Anselmo and Lothario, two close friends who live in Florence, Italy. Anselmo marries Camilla, a beautiful woman who has the purest intentions. One day Anselmo tells Lothario he wants to test Camilla's purity and chastity. He asks Lothario to woo Camilla to see whether she will be able to resist. Lothario, in a lengthy speech filled with sonnets and classical references, tells Anselmo that his plan is stupid, but Anselmo does not listen.

Lothario falsely tells Anselmo, on several occasions, that he has tried and failed to woo Camilla. Anselmo spies on the two of them and realizes that Lothario has been lying to him—he has not made any false advances toward Camilla. Anselmo makes Lothario swear that he will try to woo Camilla while Anselmo is away for a week on a business trip. Lothario does try to woo Camilla and inadvertently falls in love with her. Camilla sends a letter to Anselmo begging him to come home and rescue her from his deceitful friend Lothario.

Chapter XXXIV

Anselmo receives Camilla's letter, realizes that his plan is working, and refuses to come home early. Over time Camilla succumbs to Lothario's advances and they begin a love affair. When Anselmo returns, Lothario tells him that Camilla has resisted his seduction. Anselmo adds to the plan by asking Lothario to write love poetry for Camilla, which the lovestruck Lothario is now thrilled to do. Camilla's maid, Leonela, helps Lothario and Camilla carry on their affair and takes a lover of her own. Though worried that Leonela will bring her shame, Camilla does not interfere because she fears Leonela will tell Anselmo about her affair with Lothario.

One morning, Lothario sees Leonela's lover leaving the house and thinks Camilla has taken another lover. In a fit of jealous rage, he tells Anselmo that he has seduced Camilla but that she has not yet acted on her love for him. Lothario reveals Camilla's plan to meet him in a closet on a certain day and encourages Anselmo to observe his wife's infidelity. In the meantime, Camilla tells Lothario of her concerns about Leonela, prompting Lothario to realize his mistake. He tells her about his blunder, and she forms a plan to trick Anselmo so that she and Lothario can carry out their affair in the open. She meets Lothario in the closet and, aware that Anselmo is watching, pretends to stab herself rather than give up her purity to Lothario. The deception works, enabling Camilla to carry on her affair with Lothario without Anselmo ever suspecting.

Chapter XXXV

While the priest is reading, Sancho rushes into the room to tell everyone that Don Quixote has slain the giant who captured Dorothea's kingdom. Rushing to see what has happened, they find that Don Quixote is battling the giant in his sleep and has destroyed several of the innkeeper's wineskins, which Sancho has mistaken for a giant's head. When Sancho cannot find the giant's head, he becomes crazed, fearing that he will not get his governorship.

The priest finishes reading the story contained in the manuscript. Anselmo discovers Leonela's affair. To prevent Anselmo from killing her, Leonela promises to tell him something very important the next morning. When Anselmo tells Camilla about his discovery, she runs away to

Lothario's, afraid that Leonela will reveal their affair to Anselmo. Camilla and Lothario flee. When Anselmo wakes the next morning, Leonela has run away. Not finding Camilla either, Anselmo goes to Lothario's for help and discovers that Lothario too has left. On the way to another friend's house, he learns of Lothario and Camilla's treachery from a traveler. Reaching his friend's house, Anselmo dies of grief from the loss of his honor. The priest announces that he likes the manuscript but finds it impossible to believe that a husband could be so stupid.

Chapter XXXVI
Ferdinand and Lucinda arrive at the inn in disguise. After a tearful scene, Ferdinand reunites with Dorothea, and Cardenio reunites with Lucinda. Ferdinand tells the company that he and his friends kidnapped Lucinda from the convent where she stayed after running away from the wedding. He now swears his love for Dorothea. Everyone weeps with joy except Sancho, who weeps for the loss of his kingdom now that he and Don Quixote know that Dorothea is not a princess.

Chapter XXXVII
In distress, Sancho wakes Don Quixote to tell him that Dorothea is not really a princess and that the giant he fought in his dreams was really just a wineskin. Don Quixote dismisses Sancho's news merely as further evidence of the inn's enchantment. He reassures Dorothea that he has sworn to be her protector and that it was unnecessary for her father to turn her into an ordinary maiden to protect her from the enchantment. He then tells her about his fight with the giant, but he stops mid-story, remarking that "time, which unveils all mysteries, will reveal this one when we least expect it."

Dorothea tells Don Quixote that she is still the Princess Micomicona and still needs his assistance. While Don Quixote berates Sancho for his apparent lie, a traveler dressed like a Moor—hereafter referred to as the captive—and his beautiful companion, Zoraida, arrive at the inn in search of a place to stay. The captive tells the company that Zoraida is a Moorish lady of rank who wants to be baptized. Over dinner, Don Quixote gives a speech about the relative merits of scholars and knights. He is so articulate that at that moment no one thinks he is crazy.

Analysis: XXXII–XXXVII
The section containing the reunification of the lovers provides the dramatic climax of the novel's First Part, and the fact that Don Quixote misses the action of this scene demonstrates how much his madness has alienated him from the rest of the characters. Coming as it does on the heels of the tragic ending of Anselmo's story, the reunification scene appears especially sweet, though unlikely. The capture and return of

Don Quixote to the inn is almost inconsequential in comparison, since Don Quixote continues to live on in his fantasy life. Lost in his madness, he completely misses the reunion, which represents the climax of his madness and alienation and raises doubts about his position in the novel overall. Here, Don Quixote appears to exist almost outside of the events of the novel itself, as though he were nothing more than a guide. The circumstances related to his return bring the necessary parties together, but the crux of the action in this section takes place with him outside the picture.

Just as every climax is followed by a falling action, Don Quixote's climax of madness dissipates as he gradually begins to see things for what they really are. In the incident with the wineskins, he wakes to the realization that others do not believe him. He refrains from telling Dorothea about slaying the giant out of an awareness that she will not believe him. He then shocks the crowd with the clarity and sanity of his speech, which lauds the virtues of knights over those of scholars. His understanding that others think he is crazy continues to grow throughout the novel, although at any given moment this awareness ebbs and flows. At this point in the novel, his awareness keeps his madness in check, since his madness has grown to such an extent that he is in danger of falling out of his own story.

The priest's reading of Anselmo's tale adds more layers to the narrative in *Don Quixote*. The manuscript, which is found in a trunk that an unknown man has left at the inn, is shrouded in so much mystery that we do not know who narrates the story. Furthermore, the story, written in a high style with long and improbable speeches, seems to be fictional rather than historical. Despite its alleged falsehood, however, the tale is more plausible than many of the stories in the novel that the characters insist are true. It is certainly more plausible than the scene in which the lovers reunite, a scene that Cervantes heralds as true to life. The priest's observation that Anselmo's story cannot be true because a husband would never be that stupid is ironic. Compared with the unlikely reunion of the four lovers in *Don Quixote,* the stupidity Anselmo displays in the story is plausible.

THE FIRST PART, CHAPTERS XXXVIII–XLV

CHAPTER XXXVIII
Don Quixote continues his lecture on the superiority of knights over scholars. Everyone is impressed with his intelligence, but still no one believes that chivalry is more important than scholarship. The captive begins to tell the story of his imprisonment and rescue in Moorish lands.

Chapter XXXIX

The captive tells the group that he left home many years earlier after his father divided the family estate and ordered his three sons to leave home to become a soldier, a priest, and a sailor, respectively. He gives a lengthy account of the wars in which he has fought. The captive mentions that he fought alongside Don Pedro de Aguilar, Ferdinand's brother.

Chapter XL

The captive recounts his capture and imprisonment in Algiers. One day he was on the roof of the prison when Zoraida, who had fallen in love with him from afar, dropped some money to him from a window. Along with the money, she included a letter that said she had converted to Christianity and that offered him financial assistance to escape, free her, and bring her to Spain to be his wife. The captive used Zoraida's money to ransom himself and some of his fellow prisoners, buy a boat, and make arrangements to free Zoraida from her father's home.

Chapter XLI

The captive says that he snuck into Zoraida's father's garden to see her, told her of his plan to escape from Algiers, and finally kidnapped her. Zoraida's father awoke while the captive was kidnapping her, so they brought the father with them on the ship and dropped him off some miles away from the city. The captive and his companions rowed for several days until French pirates robbed them of all Zoraida's riches. Once they arrived in Spain, they determined to go to the captive's father, baptize Zoraida, and get married.

Chapter XLII

After the captive finishes his story, a judge named Licentiate Juan Perez de Viedma arrives at the inn with his beautiful daughter, Clara. The captive realizes that the judge is his brother. The priest, after successfully testing the judge to see whether he still loves his missing brother, reunites the two. While everyone sleeps that night, a youth sings love ballads outside the inn. Cardenio creeps into the women's room to tell them to listen.

Chapter XLIII

Dorothea wakes Clara so she can hear the singing, saying it is the most beautiful singing she has ever heard. Clara reveals that the singing youth is actually a young lord who used to live with his father next door to her and the judge. Clara adds that he has followed her in disguise because he is in love with her. She and the young lord have never spoken, but she loves him and wishes to marry him. Dorothea promises to try to arrange for Clara to speak with him.

Meanwhile, Don Quixote stands guard outside the inn. The inn-keeper's daughter and her maid, Maritornes, fool him into giving them his hand through a window. They tie his hand to a door and leave him standing in his stirrups on Rocinante's back for the night. Four horsemen arrive and mock Don Quixote as they try to enter the inn.

CHAPTER XLIV

Don Quixote makes such a racket that the innkeeper comes out to see what is going on. The horsemen are servants to the father of Don Louis, the young lord in love with Clara. The four horsemen find Don Louis and order him to come home with them, but he refuses. The judge takes Don Louis aside and asks him why he refuses to return home. Meanwhile, two guests attempt to leave the inn without paying, and the innkeeper fights them. Don Quixote refuses to assist the innkeeper because he has sworn not to engage in any new adventures until he has slain the giant who captured Dorothea's kingdom.

Cervantes returns to the conversation between Don Louis and the judge. Don Louis tells the judge of his love for Clara and begs for her hand in marriage. The judge says he will consider the proposal. Meanwhile, Don Quixote, through words alone, has successfully persuaded the two guests to quit beating the innkeeper. A barber—the same one from whom Don Quixote earlier steals the basin that he believes is Mambrino's helmet—arrives at the inn. The barber accuses Don Quixote and Sancho of theft, but Sancho defends them by claiming that Don Quixote vanquished the barber and took the items as spoils of war.

CHAPTER XLV

The people at the inn play along with Don Quixote's insistence that the basin is actually Mambrino's helmet. A huge fight breaks out, but Don Quixote finally ends the brawl by asking the priest and the judge to calm everyone. The judge decides to bring Don Louis to Andalusia along with him and Clara, and he tells the servants about his plan. A member of the Holy Brotherhood, attracted to the scene by the outbreak of violence, realizes that he has a warrant for Don Quixote's arrest for freeing the galley slaves. Don Quixote laughs at the man and rails about the stupidity of trying to arrest a knight-errant.

ANALYSIS: XXXVIII–XLV

The captive's tale and the story of Clara and Don Louis demonstrate that at least several of Don Quixote's contemporaries share one of his most insane features—unfailing romantic idealization of women they do not even know. With the exception of Dorothea, the women in the First Part of *Don Quixote* are weak-willed, subservient creatures who rely on their husbands as masters. In the novel, men revere women for their beauty and their chastity, but women remain mere objects over whom men fight or drive themselves insane. Even Dorothea ingratiates and humiliates herself in order to win back Ferdinand's affection, which seems to be little more than lust. In order to rebel, the women must dress as men and run away from home, but even then they remain frightened young maidens stranded in situations largely beyond their control. Zoraida stands out as the one seeming exception to this model, since she has the will to steal from her father in order to run away from home with the captive. As a Moor, she can step outside the bounds of the conventional roles governing the lives of Cervantes's women, just as the character Anna Felix is able to do late in the Second Part. Nonetheless, we never hear Zoraida speak, and this muteness symbolizes her lack of power. Therefore, even though her ethnicity and religious passion make her unusual and suggest that she might serve as the model for a new kind of woman in the narrative, she remains an object and a marginalized figure.

With the story of the captive and Zoraida, Cervantes provides a largely autobiographical account of his life in captivity. Cervantes tried to escape captivity in Algiers three times before he was finally ransomed. The fanciful escape of the captive may, then, represent one of Cervantes's fantasies. The detailed account of the war in which the captive fought is merely a soldier's account of important historical events, nothing more. It bears no relation to the actual characters or events of the novel and therefore stands out as material related more to Cervantes's life than to the story in progress.

Class distinctions come into sharp focus at the inn. The captive and Zoraida, who are nobles motivated only by the loftiest intentions, succeed in their crazy scheme to get back to Spain. The lower class characters, on the other hand, become embroiled in various skirmishes. The innkeeper is forced to squabble with two guests over payment for the night's lodgings, while Sancho and the traveling barber brawl over a harness. The wickedness of the innkeeper's daughter contrasts sharply with the goodness of Clara, the noble judge's daughter, highlighting the difference in their social station. Even Don Quixote preserves the standards of his day, upholding the virtues of the aristocrats and condemning the insolence of the poor. He finds Sancho's impertinence unbearable when it seems to impinge upon his sense of nobility.

THE FIRST PART, CHAPTERS XLVI–LII

CHAPTER XLVI

The priest pacifies the members of the Holy Brotherhood by convincing them that Don Quixote is insane and should not be held accountable for his actions. Still under the impression that Dorothea is the Princess Micomicona, Don Quixote tells her that the time has come to continue their journey to her kingdom so that he may slay the giant. Sancho objects, telling everyone that he has seen Dorothea kissing Ferdinand and that she cannot, therefore, be a princess.

Don Quixote is infuriated by Sancho's insolence, but Dorothea pacifies him by telling him that Sancho must have been subject to an enchantment that made him believe he saw her kissing Ferdinand. Don Quixote forgives Sancho, who says he believes that the inn must be enchanted because of all the bizarre things that have happened. Sancho adds, however, that he is still certain that the blanket-tossing he received there was an act committed by real people. Don Quixote assures Sancho that the blanket-tossing was an enchantment as well, which is why Don Quixote has not avenged it. Sancho does not believe him.

The barber and priest contrive a plan to get Don Quixote back to their village without the help of Dorothea and Ferdinand. They build a cage, capture Don Quixote, bind him, and place him in the cage on the back of an ox cart. The barber then pretends to be a sage and predicts Don Quixote's valorous return to his village and his reunion and marriage to Dulcinea.

Chapter XLVII
Don Quixote accepts the enchantment that he believes is afflicting him but wonders why he travels so slowly. He concludes that enchantments must have changed since the old days, when knights were whisked away on clouds and traveled at very high speeds. Sancho warns Don Quixote that he is not enchanted, but Don Quixote does not believe him. As the group leaves, the innkeeper gives the priest some papers from the trunk the unknown man left at the inn. The priest is anxious to read them.

On the road, the group meets another priest, a canon of Toledo, who rides with the group for a while to talk to the priest from Don Quixote's hometown. Sancho challenges the barber, saying that he knows that the barber and the priest have taken Don Quixote captive. The barber threatens to lock Sancho in the cage too, and Sancho becomes indignant. The canon tells the priest that he considers books of chivalry to be ridiculous lies and harmful to the populace. He also berates the style of chivalric books, saying that they should all be banished. The priest says he agrees for the most part but that he is able to appreciate them.

Chapter XLVIII
The canon says he began writing a book of chivalry but stopped because he discovered that an author must write either good books that the crowds dislike or low-quality books that displease the critics. He then rails against the state of theater in Spain and suggests that there should be a government official to oversee decisions about which plays get produced and which do not. Sancho tells Don Quixote that the barber and the priest have been faking his enchantment out of jealousy of his great

deeds. Sancho asks Don Quixote whether he needs to use the bathroom; Don Quixote replies that he does.

CHAPTER XLIX
Sancho tells Don Quixote that since enchanted people have no bodily needs, Don Quixote's need to use the bathroom proves that he is not enchanted. Don Quixote responds that there are new kinds of enchantment but promises nonetheless to try to free himself. When the party stops for lunch, the priest lets Don Quixote out of the cage, and he and the canon argue about chivalry. The canon marvels that Don Quixote mingles fact and fiction with no concern for the difference.

CHAPTER L
Don Quixote tells the story of the Knight of the Lake, a fantasy story of enchantment that, he claims, proves the delightful and fascinating nature of stories of knight-errantry. Don Quixote also tells the canon that since becoming a knight-errant he himself has been brave, courteous, and well-bred, enduring many adventures and enchantments.

A goatherd appears, chasing a goat that has wandered into the group's picnic. The group is amused that the goatherd speaks to the animal. The goatherd then tells the group that he is a peasant but that he knows how to converse with both men and beasts. The priest says that he is not surprised.

CHAPTER LI
The goatherd, whose name is Eugenio, tells the group that he and his friend Anselmo have been driven to the simple life of shepherds by Leandra, a beautiful, wealthy young woman from their town. Leandra ran away with an arrogant soldier who then robbed her and abandoned her in a cave in the woods. Eugenio tells the group that the woods in the area ring with sounds of the sobbing shepherds who are in love with Leandra. Leandra's father put her in a convent in hopes that over time she would recover her honor.

CHAPTER LII
The goatherd insults Don Quixote and the two of them brawl as the others cheer them on. Don Quixote then sees a group of penitents carrying an icon of the blessed Virgin Mary, on their way to pray for rain. Thinking that the penitents are rogues who have captured a lady, he attacks them and gets a beating from one of them. Sancho thinks Don Quixote has died and mourns his friend in a particularly eloquent elegy. Sancho's words stir Don Quixote, who agrees to go home until his luck changes.

When Don Quixote and Sancho arrive home, Sancho's wife (now called Juana), asks him what he has brought her. He puts her off, promising that he will soon be made a governor and that he has tales that will surely amuse her for now. Don Quixote's niece and housekeeper welcome him home but worry about his madness. They fear he will disappear again, which, Cervantes tells us, he will.

Cervantes ends the narration by saying that he searched far and wide for more manuscripts about Don Quixote but that he was unable to find them until he met an aged doctor who found a leaden box in the remains of an ancient hermitage. The box contained several parchments with sonnets and epitaphs to Don Quixote, Sancho, and Dulcinea, which Cervantes reproduced. Finally, he tells us that, at great cost to himself, he has found an account of the third expedition of Don Quixote and hopes to publish it.

ANALYSIS: CHAPTERS XLVI–LII

The priest proves to be a muddled character in this section, as we see his mixed opinion about stories of chivalry and his mixed reaction to Don Quixote's madness. When the priest takes the manuscripts from the innkeeper to read—just as when he reads aloud Anselmo's story and when he preserves several of the novels in Don Quixote's library—he shows his unwillingness to purge all tales of chivalry from the world. As much as he rails against the tales as harmful to the general public, it is plain that he enjoys them. In his conversation with the canon, the priest reveals an attachment to the author's craft that exceeds his apparent disdain for the tales' inaccuracy. The priest's attitude toward his friend Don Quixote is likewise inconsistent. On the one hand, he berates Don Quixote for Don Quixote's insanity and leads the attempt to bring him home and cure him. On the other hand, however, he apparently enjoys his prank, playing along by caging Don Quixote and telling him that he is under an enchantment. The priest's alternating attitudes reveal a human affection for books and imagination, even as he outwardly claims to reject both on intellectual grounds.

Cervantes has often been criticized for the insensitivity shown by the group that watches the fight between Don Quixote and the goatherd in Chapter LII. The cheering by the priest and the others—as though they are at a dogfight—suggests that, on a certain level, they consider Don Quixote to be no more than an animal. They first laugh at his madness and then condescend to him by playing along with the idea of the enchantment. Here, they view him as nothing more than a creature for their enjoyment, manipulating him to suit their purposes, sometimes at great physical cost to him. In this regard, the priest's and the barber's interest in bringing Don Quixote home safely and curing him is bizarre and inexplicable. One possibility is that the two men are acting out of concern for Don Quixote's niece and housekeeper, who genuinely seem to care for Don Quixote.

The unfriendly motivations of those who lead Don Quixote back to his home affect Don Quixote, causing him to lose sight of his goals and ideals. At the end of the First Part, Don Quixote nearly relinquishes his chivalric ideals without replacing them with anything of equal value or passion. He appears to be deceived about his enchantment to the end, eventually conceding to go home. He explains that he will rest at home until his foul luck has passed, but he makes no mention of his vow to Dorothea or his love for Dulcinea. This listless quality is not in keeping with his characteristic stubborn insistence on formalities and vows. The end of the First Part is therefore abrupt and somewhat unsatisfying to those who appreciate Don Quixote's spirit and passion. Nonetheless, his decline appears reasonable in light of the ill intentions and petty desires of those around him on his journey home. Sancho stands out from the others, however, as someone who continues to care about Don Quixote. Despite Sancho's self-serving intentions, he displays an honest interest in his friend.

THE SECOND PART, THE AUTHOR'S DEDICATION OF THE SECOND PART–CHAPTER VII

THE AUTHOR'S DEDICATION OF THE SECOND PART
Cervantes offers his novel to the Count of Lemos, saying that he is sending Don Quixote back out into the world to "purge the disgust and nausea caused by another Don Quixote who has been running about the world masquerading as the Second Part." Cervantes says he rejected an offer from the emperor of China to be the rector of a college of Castilian language in which *The History of Don Quixote* would be the primary textbook. Because the emperor did not send an advance, Cervantes sent his envoy away and decided to commend his work to the Count of Lemos.

PROLOGUE
Cervantes introduces the Second Part, the account of the third expedition of Don Quixote, by railing against an author who has published a false sequel to the First Part of *Don Quixote*. Cervantes suggests that if readers run into that author, they should tell him a story about a man who, using a hollow cane, inflated a dog to the astonishment of bystanders. The man's response to his audience's questioning was to ask them whether they think it is an easy thing to blow up a dog.

Cervantes also wants the reader to pass on an anecdote about a man who carried around a heavy slab that he drops on dogs in the street. One day, a dog owner beats the man, making him too afraid to drop slabs on any more dogs. Cervantes suggests the author should be likewise afraid to publish any more bad books. Cervantes defends his honor against the personal slights the other author has made, saying that although he may be poor and a cripple, he has earned his wounds in battle and is proud of them.

CHAPTER I

Cervantes tells us that Cide Hamete Benengeli continues his account of Don Quixote's adventures by recounting the priest and the barber's visit to Don Quixote after a month of not seeing him. Don Quixote initially seems sane, but when the priest gets him started talking about chivalry, it becomes clear that Don Quixote has not given up his intention of being a knight-errant.

CHAPTER II

Sancho comes to visit Don Quixote to find out when they will again embark on their quest for adventure, but the niece and the housekeeper try to keep Sancho out of the house. Don Quixote orders them to let Sancho in and then asks Sancho about Don Quixote's reputation in the village. Sancho tells him that many consider him mad. He then tells Don Quixote about the publication of a book of their previous adventures. The book contains so many details that Sancho marvels that the writer could have learned about all of them. Don Quixote thinks that the writer is a sage enchanter, but Sancho says the writer is a Moor whose name is Cide Hamete Aubergine. Sancho goes to the village to find the student Sampson Carrasco, from whom he has heard about the book.

CHAPTER III

While Sancho fetches Sampson, Don Quixote muses that the Moorish enchanter who wrote the book must either want to tear him down or exalt him. He laments that the author is a Moor because he does not believe that Moors ever tell the truth. Sampson arrives and tells Don Quixote about the book and its author, Cide Hamete Benengeli. He also mentions that the book has been translated into Christian tongues. Sampson criticizes the novel for the anecdotal digressions in which Don Quixote plays no part but says that everyone enjoys reading the novel nonetheless. He also mentions several textual inconsistencies regarding the appearance and disappearance of Dapple. Sancho says he can explain those inconsistencies but runs off with a stomachache.

CHAPTER IV

Sancho returns and explains that a thief stole Dapple from him when he was strung up. Sampson says that Sancho's explanation does not justify the inconsistencies in the book, and Sancho replies that perhaps the author or the printer made an error. He explains how he spent the hundred crowns he found in the saddlebags in the Sierra Morena, and Sampson promises to tell the author so that he can revise the book. Sampson says that the author promises to publish the Second Part when he finds the manuscript. Sampson then tells Don Quixote about a jousting festival in Saragossa and suggests that he seek fame there. Don Quixote begs Sampson to write a poem in which each line begins with a letter of Dulcinea's name.

CHAPTER V

Cervantes tells us that "the translator" doubts that this chapter is authentic because it seems impossible that Sancho would have spoken in such a high style. Cervantes does not identify this translator. Sancho goes home to Teresa—whose name at the end of the First Part is Juana—and tells her that he will soon be leaving with Don Quixote on another adventure. Teresa warns Sancho not to dream too much and to be content with his station. Sancho replies that he wants to marry off his daughter and make her a countess. Teresa objects to this plan, saying that people are happier when they marry within their own class.

CHAPTER VI

The niece and housekeeper beg Don Quixote to stay at home. They say that if he must go he should join the king's court rather than go on more adventures. Don Quixote insists that he must do what he was born to do and pursue his life as a knight-errant. He discusses honor and pedigree, claiming that he knows of only two ways to increase fame and honor—through arms or letters—and that he has chosen arms.

CHAPTER VII

Distressed at Don Quixote's madness, the housekeeper begs Sampson to speak with him. Sancho visits Don Quixote, and they discuss Teresa's advice and her wish that Sancho receive wages from Don Quixote. Don Quixote refuses to fix Sancho's wages and tells him to stay home if he does not have the strength to be a squire. Sancho weeps and promises to come along. Sampson too visits Don Quixote, but instead of dissuading him from his journey, Sampson encourages him to embark at once. Cervantes alludes to a plan Sampson has developed with the priest and the barber and says that the plan will be detailed later in the history.

ANALYSIS: DEDICATION–CHAPTER VII

Cervantes's mention of the imposter who publishes the false sequel of the story makes the novel more self-referential. In real life, an author by the name of Avellaneda wrote a false sequel to *Don Quixote* that appeared several years after the original publishing of the First Part of *Don Quixote*, in 1604. This false sequel not only inspired Cervantes to hurry along his own sequel, which he published in 1614, but it altered the context of that text. Cervantes chose to mention the false sequel in his fictional tale, further blurring the line between the novel's fictional and historical aspects.

On the one hand, we can argue that the story of Don Quixote remains fictional. In the First Part, the only person who speaks of Cide Hamete Benengeli is Cervantes himself. It is logical for Cervantes to be the only one to do so, since if Cide Hamete Benengeli did indeed originate the tale, as Cervantes claims he did, then the characters in the tale would not be able to speak about him as their author. However, the world of the novel in the Second Part is not logical, and Sancho refers directly to Cide Hamete Benengeli. Therefore, if we still have any doubts about the tongue-in-cheek nature of Cervantes's initial claim that he is writing from the historical manuscript of Cide Hamete Benengeli, we can put those doubts to rest. One could argue that in the decade that passed between the publication of the First Part and the Second Part, the characters, if they were historical personages, would have been able, in real life, to find out about Benengeli, Avellaneda, and even Cervantes. But the Second Part picks up only one month—not years—after the end of the First Part. Nevertheless, Sancho later writes a letter to his wife and dates it 1614, the year the Second Part was published. Because of the deep correlation between the actual, historical publication of the novel and the story it contains, this letter should also date the first half of the novel as 1614, but we know that it was published in 1604. This discrepancy emphasizes the novel's fictional nature.

The concept of authorship, especially as it relates to Don Quixote's control of his own fate, plays a large role in the Second Part. The idea of vague authorship illuminates the conflict between the imaginary world and the real one, a conflict that Don Quixote himself embodies. Essentially, Cervantes allows the characters to influence their own story like authors. When Don Quixote expresses his concern over the accuracy of the First Part of the novel, he, the main character of the First Part, doubts the accuracy of his own story. Moreover, despite the fact that Cervantes states in the First Part that he is the translator of Cide Hamete Benengeli's work, he now refers to an unidentified translator without providing any clues about this translator's identity. We are thus left with an even blurrier picture of the truth.

The trickery of Don Quixote's friends in this opening section reveals their desire to see Don Quixote once again go out to pursue his fantasies. The priest, who spends so much time in the First Part trying to coax Don Quixote home, delights in the fact that his friend is apparently still mad. Similarly, Sampson Carrasco's lie to the housekeeper that he will talk sense into Don Quixote exposes his knavery and his willingness to play with Don Quixote's imagination. The priest and Samson mimic Sancho, who buys into Don Quixote's whims even though he knows that his master is insane. By encouraging Don Quixote's madness, these characters reveal their own desire for adventure. They express this desire vicariously through Don Quixote.

THE SECOND PART, CHAPTERS VIII–XV

CHAPTER VIII

Cervantes says that Cide Hamete Benengeli blesses Allah before recounting that Don Quixote and Sancho once again go on the road. He begs us to forget the past adventures and pay attention only to what is to come. Don Quixote and Sancho think it a good sign that Rocinante and Dapple bray and stamp as they set out. Sancho thinks it an especially good sign that Dapple whinnies louder than Rocinante does. Cervantes interjects to say that Benengeli's history does not indicate whether Sancho's belief is based on astrology.

Don Quixote decides to go to El Toboso to visit Dulcinea. On the road, he and Sancho discuss the importance of fame. Don Quixote says that people value fame even in its negative form. Sancho says he believes they should try to become saints rather than knights because saints go to heaven. Don Quixote argues that the world already has enough saints and that he was born to be a knight-errant.

CHAPTER IX

Don Quixote and Sancho decide to enter El Toboso at night. Sancho panics because he does not know which house is Dulcinea's, even though he supposedly visited her to give her Don Quixote's letter in the First Part. The two run into a ploughman who tells them he does not know of any princesses in the area. They go outside the town to sleep.

CHAPTER X

Cervantes says that the author, presumably Cide Hamete Benengeli, wanted to skip this chapter for fear that he would not be believed but decided to write it anyhow. Don Quixote dispatches Sancho to fetch Dulcinea and bring her to him. Sancho panics because he has never seen Dulcinea and fears he will be attacked if people see him wandering around the town looking for women.

Sancho sits down for a while and has a lengthy dialogue with himself. He concludes that he can fool Don Quixote by abducting the first peasant girl he sees riding on the road and presenting her as Dulcinea. Sancho sees three young peasant girls riding. Cervantes says that the author does not clarify whether these girls are riding on horses or donkeys. Sancho rushes to Don Quixote and informs him that Dulcinea is approaching with two maids on horseback, but Don Quixote objects that he can see merely three peasants on donkeys.

As the girls ride by, Sancho grabs one of them and falls down on his knees before her, praising her as Dulcinea. Though appalled by her appearance—and especially by her smell—Don Quixote believes that she is Dulcinea. He says that a wicked enchanter who wants to deny him the pleasure of seeing Dulcinea's beauty has changed her into a peasant.

Sancho describes Dulcinea to Don Quixote as he claims he saw her, including a mole with seven or eight nine-inch hairs coming out of it.

CHAPTER XI
On the road, Don Quixote and Sancho encounter a wagon filled with actors in costume. Don Quixote stops to speak to them, but one of the costumes frightens Rocinante and the horse throws Don Quixote to the ground. One of the actors imitates Don Quixote's antics by stealing Dapple and reenacting the scene. Don Quixote rides Rocinante up to the wagon to avenge the injury but stops short when he sees the whole company lined up in the road, armed with rocks. Sancho talks his master out of attacking the group, pointing out that the actors are not knights and that they returned Dapple unharmed.

CHAPTER XII
While sleeping in a grove, Don Quixote and Sancho meet another knight who claims to be pining away for his mistress, Casildea de Vandalia, to whom he recites poetry. The narrator calls him the Knight of the Wood and calls his squire the Squire of the Wood. Sancho and the Squire of the Wood go off into the night to talk while Don Quixote and the Knight of the Wood stay where they are to talk.

CHAPTER XIII
Sancho and the Squire of the Wood eat and drink while discussing their shared expectation that their masters will make each of them a governor of an isle. They also tell each other about their children. Sancho laments Don Quixote's madness but says that he is honest and pure, unlike the Knight of the Wood, who, according to the Squire of the Wood, is quite a rogue. Sancho declares that he is a great taster of wines, and the two of them drink until they pass out, still holding the wine flask.

CHAPTER XIV
Meanwhile, Don Quixote and the Knight of the Wood discuss their knightly adventures. The Knight of the Wood tells Don Quixote that his lady has sent him into the world to make all knights proclaim her beauty. He says that his greatest conquest was his defeat of Don Quixote de la Mancha. Don Quixote tells the Knight that this cannot be possible and challenges him to a duel. The Knight of the Wood accepts but says that they must wait until morning. They rouse Sancho and the Squire of the Wood, who discuss whether they too should fight.

At dawn, Sancho sees the Squire of the Wood's nose and becomes so frightened by its size that he scurries up a tree before the duel. The Knight of the Wood dresses in such fine, shiny material that he is renamed the Knight of the Mirrors, but he refuses to show Don Quixote his face. Don Quixote pauses to help Sancho into the tree, throwing off the timing of the duel. As a result, the Knight of the Mirrors cannot get his horse going again fast enough, enabling Don Quixote to knock him off his horse quite easily. Don Quixote removes the Knight of the Mirrors's visor, revealing Sampson Carrasco. Don Quixote does not believe that Sampson stands before him; he thinks that he is still under an enchantment. The Squire of the Wood removes his pasteboard nose and reveals himself as Thomas Cecial, Sancho's neighbor. Sampson confesses Dulcinea's beauty, and Don Quixote spares him.

CHAPTER XV

Sampson reveals that he has been plotting with the priest and the barber to vanquish Don Quixote and to order him to go home for two years. Samson's squire leaves him, but Samson vows revenge on Don Quixote.

ANALYSIS: CHAPTERS VIII–XV

Sancho's trickery in the incident with the peasant women and Sampson's deception about his identity emphasize the willingness of Don Quixote's peers to engage him in his world of deception and fantasy. Sancho is motivated by self-interest, whereas other characters play along due either to a desire to help Don Quixote or a need for a diversion. In all cases, Don Quixote's imagination shapes the novel's plot. Don Quixote's dreams direct the actions of other characters, just as they do when Dorothea pretends to be a princess in the First Part. This playfulness influences the characters' interactions with Don Quixote throughout the remainder of the novel.

The costumes worn by the actors on the wagon and by the Knight of the Mirrors show that the physical world has begun to imitate Don Quixote's fantasies. Previously, Don Quixote misperceives everything around him, seeing windmills as giants and prostitutes as princesses. Now, however, the physical world has become difficult for anyone to define clearly. Rocinante, mistaking the costumed actor for an apparition, is terrified. Moreover, the Knight of the Wood becomes known as the Knight of the Mirrors in the middle of the chapter due to his change in appearance. Cervantes now mixes reality with elements of deception, which validates Don Quixote's misperceptions and makes him seem more sane. Whereas earlier it is easy to perceive Don Quixote as insane, it now seems that the world around him is illogical. As a result, Don Quixote becomes more of a driving force in the novel, almost as though his fantasies have begun to dictate the course of the physical world around him.

Cervantes brings up religion by mentioning Benengeli's praise of Allah and Sancho's suggestion that he and Don Quixote try to become saints. The novel repeatedly touches on the importance of being a Christian in Cervantes's Spain. Cervantes often brings up religion in reference to Sancho, who Cervantes says is an old Christian and whose wise aphorisms often stem from Christian sources. The captive's earlier tale about the Moor Zoraida's passionate longing to convert to Christiantity and subsequent baptism makes Zoraida appear to be a good and beautiful woman. This depiction of the essential goodness within Zoraida despite her Moorish heritage contrasts with Cervantes's and his characters' dismissal of her Moorish countrymen as liars and cheats. Moreover, in the discussion on the way to Chrysostom's funeral, in Chapter XIII, Don Quixote compromises his extreme faith in chivalric traditions in order to allow knights-errant to praise God. Christianity, then, unlike most of the social customs of the times, receives a positive and somber treatment in the novel and stands alone as the one major subject Cervantes does not treat with a mordant, ironic tone. Here, at the beginning of the third expedition, Cervantes treats Christianity with more reverence than at any other point in the novel.

THE SECOND PART, CHAPTERS XVI–XXI

CHAPTER XVI

Sancho is confused about the identity of the Squire of the Wood and the Knight of the Mirrors. Don Quixote tries to convince him that the Squire of the Wood is not Sancho's neighbor but rather an enchantment, just as the Knight of the Wood is an enchantment that took the form of Sampson in an attempt to force Don Quixote's mercy. Sancho, who knows that the supposed enchantment of Dulcinea was a deception, does not know what to think now.

On the road, Don Quixote and Sancho meet Don Diego de Miranda, a gentleman dressed all in green. Don Quixote introduces himself to Don Diego and tells him about the history that was written about his first adventures. Don Diego marvels that knights-errant still roam the land and is glad to hear about the book, which he thinks might correct all the nonsense written in books of chivalry. Don Diego describes his life. Sancho begins to think the man is a saint and kisses his foot. Don Diego tells Don Quixote about his son, who abandoned the sciences in favor of poetry. Don Quixote responds with an eloquent speech about the value of poetry, which he compares to a delicate maiden. As they talk, Sancho wanders over to some shepherds to beg for milk.

CHAPTER XVII

Don Quixote sees a cart coming toward him hung with the king's flags, and he senses another adventure. He summons Sancho, who puts the curds he just bought from the shepherds into Don Quixote's helmet. When Don Quixote puts on the helmet, the curds run down his face, and he thinks that his brain is melting. When he recognizes the curds in the helmet, he accuses Sancho of foul play, but Sancho replies that an enchanter must have put them there.

Don Quixote hails the cart. The mule driver tells him that the cart carries two lions for the king. Don Quixote challenges the lions, and despite everyone's protests, he insists on having the cage opened. Cervantes interjects that Cide Hamete Benengeli extols Don Quixote's bravery before continuing the narrative. The others run away and the lion tamer opens the cage. Don Quixote faces the lions with "childish bravado," but the lion just stretches and lies down again. Don Quixote decides not to provoke the lions. He calls the others back, and the lion tamer recounts the story of Don Quixote's valor. Don Quixote tells Sancho to give the mule driver and the lion tamer some money for their troubles and renames himself the Knight of the Lions. Don Quixote declares that he is not as insane as he may seem—that it is better for a knight to err on the side of courage than on the side of cowardice. Don Diego invites Don Quixote and Sancho to his home, and Don Quixote accepts.

Chapter XVIII
Don Quixote receives a warm welcome at Don Diego's home, where he meets Don Diego's son, Don Lorenzo, and asks him about his poetry. Don Lorenzo answers him, all the while wondering to himself whether Don Quixote is mad. After discussing the merits of poetry, Don Lorenzo decides that Don Quixote is indeed a madman, but a brave one with a keen intelligence. Don Lorenzo recites some poetry for Don Quixote, who says it is the best that he has ever heard. Don Lorenzo is flattered despite his belief that Don Quixote is insane. Don Quixote stays with Don Diego for four days and then sets out in search of more adventures.

Chapter XIX
Don Quixote and Sancho meet some students and peasants on their way to the wedding of Quiteria the fair and Camacho the rich. The students tell Don Quixote about Quiteria and a man named Basilio who is in love with her. They say Quiteria is marrying Camacho only because of his wealth. In the course of the discussion, two of the students quarrel about the merits of studying swordplay and challenge each other to a duel in which Don Quixote acts as umpire. The more advanced student prevails, proving, according to the narrator, that skill always prevails over strength. The group arrives at the village in the middle of the night, but Don Quixote insists on sleeping outside the village in the fields.

Chapter XX
Don Quixote and Sancho arrive at the wedding, which the narrator describes in great detail. Sancho praises Quiteria for marrying for wealth rather than love, but Don Quixote does not.

Chapter XXI
Quiteria and Camacho arrive at the wedding. Basilio shows up and throws himself on his dagger. With his dying breath, he refuses to con-

fess himself to God unless Quiteria will marry him. Quiteria agrees. Basilio reveals that it is a trick—he has not stabbed himself at all. A brawl ensues. Don Quixote halts it, announcing that no one has the right to fight over wrongs committed in the name of love. Basilio and Quiteria remain married, and Camacho takes satisfaction in the idea that Quiteria would always have loved Basilio anyway. Don Quixote and Sancho leave the party to accompany the newlyweds.

ANALYSIS: CHAPTERS XVI–XXI

Don Quixote is a changed man in the Second Part of the novel. He is milder and wiser, less belligerent, less gullible, and more compassionate toward those he meets. The incident with the lions exemplifies this change in his nature, since he neither attacks the mule-driver for contradicting him nor insists on provoking the lion. The Don Quixote of the First Part would almost certainly do both. Don Quixote's discussion with Don Lorenzo about poetry reveals a deep intellect that rarely shows itself directly in the First Part. Much like his master, Sancho also matures into a wiser and fuller character. In this second part, we learn about Sancho's family, fears, vanities, and greedy and gluttonous nature but also see his fidelity to Don Quixote. Both Don Quixote and Sancho more frequently engage in conversations with other characters, fleshing out the deeper aspects of their personalities.

Whereas Don Quixote often appears alienated from the main plot in the First Part, in the Second Part he remains involved in the action even when the action imitates the style of the First Part. Even Camacho's wedding, one of the few events in the Second Part that strongly recalls the First Part, does not alienate Don Quixote. As in each of the subplots in the First Part, Cervantes presents the relevant characters, whose lives prove important because they influence the outcome of the novel and inform its major themes. Camacho's wedding raises questions about the supremacy of love—one of Don Quixote's obsessions—and about the wisdom of stepping outside class distinctions, an issue that figures prominently in Sancho's governorship later in the Second Part. Don Quixote's quelling of the brawl by nonviolent means involves him in the event and illustrates a change in him that is consistent with his maturation. Camacho's wedding bears directly on Don Quixote's character and plot advancement, unlike, for example, Anselmo's story or even the captive's tale in the First Part. The Second Part, on the whole, is more fluid than the First Part precisely because Don Quixote involves himself in the events.

In these chapters, we see that Cide Hamete Benengeli's perspective on Don Quixote's actions begins to differ from Cervantes's. Benengeli's praise of Don Quixote's bravery in the battle with the lions, for instance, contrasts with Cervantes's own reference to Don Quixote's "childish bravado." These competing authorial perspectives highlight the underlying need for us, as readers, to judge Don Quixote's fantasies by ourselves. In the Second Part, as characters start to modify their behavior according to Don Quixote's ideas and as Don Quixote's antics impact the other characters less harshly, Cervantes emphasizes the positive sides of Don Quixote's faith against the backdrop of an outdated moral system. Whereas Don Quixote's personality is dangerously anachronistic earlier in the novel, it now appears endearing and quaint.

THE SECOND PART,
CHAPTERS XXII–XXVIII

CHAPTER XXII
Don Quixote and Sancho leave for Montesinos's Cave with Basilio's cousin, an author who writes parodies of great classical works, as a guide. When the three arrive at Montesinos's Cave, Sancho and the guide lower Don Quixote into the cave by a rope. They wait for a half hour and then pull him up, only to find him asleep.

CHAPTER XXIII
Don Quixote tells Sancho and Basilio's cousin that when he went into the cave he found a small nook and fell asleep there. When he woke up he was in a beautiful field. An old man approached him, saying that he was Montesinos under a terrible enchantment. Montesinos confirmed that he cut out the heart of Durandarte, his cousin, when Durandarte died. He took the heart to Belerma, Durandarte's wife, at Durandarte's request. But, he says, Merlin has now put all of them under a spell so that they cannot leave the cave. Durandarte lies on the ground but occasionally sighs and speaks as if he were alive. According to Montesinos, Merlin prophesied Don Quixote's coming and foresaw that Don Quixote would lift their enchantments.

Don Quixote says he was in the cave for three days and three nights and saw Dulcinea in her enchanted form there. Sancho, who knows the truth about Dulcinea's enchantment, thinks Don Quixote is crazy. Don Quixote says he understands that Sancho only speaks out against him because he loves him. Don Quixote says that Sancho will soon realize that the story is true though it may appear fantastical to him now.

CHAPTER XXIV
Cervantes says that the translator found a note from Cide Hamete Benengeli in the margin of the manuscript, warning that he believed that Don Quixote's story was not true and that, in fact, Don Quixote himself renounced it as false on his deathbed.

Basilio's cousin is thrilled by all the adventures in the cave and promises to use them in his books. Back on the road he, Don Quixote, and Sancho meet a man with a load of weapons who promises to tell them his story if they meet him at the inn where he is staying. They then meet a youth on his way to war, and Don Quixote commends the boy's bravery.

Chapter XXV

At the inn, Don Quixote meets the man with the weapons. The man tells him a story of two magistrates who lost a donkey on a mountain near his village. To recover the ass, the magistrates went around the mountain braying like asses themselves, and though they did not catch the donkey, they were very impressed with their own ability to imitate asses. Neighboring villages heard about their frivolous antics, and now each time a member of the man's village passes a member of another village, the other villager brays at him. As a result, the two villages are going to war.

Master Peter, a great and well-renowned puppeteer, arrives at the inn with an ape that whispers people's fortunes into Master Peter's ear. Sancho tries to pay Master Peter to tell what his wife is doing now, but Master Peter falls to his knees, and the ape praises Don Quixote profusely. Don Quixote is flattered but believes Master Peter has made a pact with the devil. He asks the ape whether the incident in the cave was true or false, and the ape replies that some parts were true and some false.

Chapter XXVI

Master Peter puts on a puppet show for Don Quixote. The puppet show depicts the travails of a knight who goes to rescue his wife from foreign lands. Don Quixote becomes so convinced that the show is real that he attacks and destroys the entire set. He explains that his enchanters bear responsibility for his actions because they made him believe that the puppets were real. Don Quixote pays Master Peter for his troubles nonetheless. He also treats the guests to a meal and pays the innkeeper.

Chapter XXVII

Cervantes says that Cide Hamete Benengeli swears that Master Peter is actually Gines de Pasamonte, the galley slave whom Don Quixote frees earlier near the Sierra Morena. Benengeli then returns to the narration.

Don Quixote and Sancho meet up with the army from the village whose magistrates brayed like asses. Don Quixote tries to talk the men out of attacking the other village, saying that one man cannot possibly insult an entire village. He nearly persuades the villagers and then Sancho takes over. Sancho explains that braying is nothing to be ashamed of and begins to bray himself. Thinking that Sancho is mocking them, the villagers attack him and knock him unconscious. Don Quixote runs away. The other villagers never show up to battle, so the braying village goes home victorious and happy.

Chapter XXVIII

Don Quixote berates Sancho for stupidly braying to a group of villagers already sensitive to the subject of braying. He explains that he retreated because a knight should not act out of temerity. Sancho brings up the question of his wages again, and Don Quixote gets so angry that he tries to send Sancho away. Sancho, however, apologizes.

Analysis: Chapters XXII–XXVIII

The account of Montesinos's Cave marks the high point in Don Quixote's imaginative madness. Don Quixote recounts his dream to Sancho and to Basilio's cousin with such detail and texture that, were it not for Sancho's objections, we might wonder whether the story is real. Don Quixote no longer speaks about things that other people can see and use to judge him a madman. In this instance, Don Quixote has the authority to transform a half-hour in a dark cave into three days in a crystal palace. The story, in all its fantastic detail, reveals Cervantes's talent for storytelling and stands out from the rest of the novel as a unique display of imagination and descriptive force. The description is closely modeled on Trojan hero Aeneas's encounter with Dido in the underworld in Virgil's *Aèneid*. Only Sancho, assured by the knowledge that he previously deceived Don Quixote about Dulcinea's enchantment, keeps us from believing the description completely. Nonetheless, Don Quixote's gentle, caring statement—that he understands Sancho's bewilderment but that Sancho will soon realize the truth—suddenly seems more plausible than Sancho's rational argument.

The note in the margin that Cervantes mentions in Chapter XXIV deepens the puzzle of the novel's narration by raising the question of how many translators bear responsibility for the text. In the beginning of the Second Part, Sampson tells Don Quixote that the author intends to publish a second part as soon as he finds the manuscript, which the Moor has written in his own language and an unspecified "Christian" has written in his. If the Christian is Cervantes, it is hard to explain why Cervantes refers to him throughout as "the translator." If the Christian is not Cervantes, it is hard to imagine the role Cervantes plays in bringing the novel to us. This tension and further layering of authors, narrators, and voices draws attention to the circular form of the novel, and makes Don Quixote's sanity ambiguous. We are forced to question at all times what we are reading and wonder whose perspective is most accurate.

The reappearance of Gines de Pasamonte, disguised as Master Peter, exemplifies the way the second half of the novel mirrors the first. The reappearance of characters from the first half helps join the two parts into a single novel, despite the obvious differences between them. Cervantes clearly wants to establish his work as the authentic sequel to the first half, and tying the two parts together through his characters is one way he manages to do so.

THE SECOND PART, CHAPTERS XXIX–XXXV

CHAPTER XXIX
Don Quixote and Sancho come to the river Ebro, where they find a fishing boat. Don Quixote takes the empty boat as a sign that he must use it to aid some imperiled knight. Much to Sancho's dismay, they tether Rocinante and Dapple to a tree and set off in the boat. They do not go very far, but Don Quixote believes they have traveled two thousand miles. The boat reaches some mills, where Don Quixote and Sancho nearly perish. Some of the millers save them despite the curses of Don Quixote, who believes that the millers hold a trapped knight-errant in their mill, which he calls a castle. The fisherman who owns the boat arrives, and Don Quixote pays him off.

CHAPTER XXX
In the woods, Don Quixote and Sancho encounter a Duchess hunting with a Duke. Don Quixote sends Sancho to speak with the Duchess, and she receives him favorably, since she has read the First Part of the novel. She and the Duke resolve to treat Don Quixote according to the customs in books of chivalry. After initially falling off their respective mounts, Don Quixote and Sancho ride with the Duchess and the Duke to their castle.

CHAPTER XXXI
Don Quixote, seeing that the Duke and Duchess are treating him according to chivalric traditions, feels certain that he is a true knight-errant. Sancho is also thrilled at their reception, but when he asks one of the maidservants, Doña Rodriguez, to care for Dapple, she refuses and they get into an argument. At dinner, the Duke forces Don Quixote to sit at the head of the table. Don Quixote and Sancho amuse the Duke and Duchess with their frivolity. The Duchess takes a particular liking to Sancho, who repeatedly embarrasses his master with his simplicity.

CHAPTER XXXII
Don Quixote defends knight-errantry to a clergyman who condemns it as frivolity. The Duke promises Sancho that he will make him governor of some isle, and the clergyman storms out in anger. The servants play a trick on Don Quixote by washing his head in a basin and pretending to run out of water in the middle so that he must sit at the table with a mound of suds on his head. The Duke forces them to wash his head in the same way to maintain the ruse.

The Duchess asks Don Quixote to describe Dulcinea. He says he cannot remember what Dulcinea looks like, since her memory was blotted from his mind when he saw her transformed into an ugly peasant by enchantment. The Duchess challenges Don Quixote on the fine points of his love for Dulcinea and asks how he can compare Dulcinea to other princesses when he cannot even prove that she comes from noble lineage. Don Quixote answers that Dulcinea's virtues raise her above her noble heritage. Meanwhile, Sancho goes off with the servants but comes running back in with several servants who want to clean him with dirty dishwater. Sancho implores the Duchess to intercede, which she does.

Chapter XXXIII
After dinner, the Duchess asks Sancho to accompany her to a cool place. Sancho agrees and, after making sure that the room contains no eavesdroppers, entertains her with stories of his adventures with Don Quixote. He tells her that he knows Don Quixote is crazy but that he stays with him out of loyalty. Sancho tells her how he deceived Don Quixote into believing in Dulcinea's enchantment, but the Duchess convinces Sancho that he is the one who was actually deceived. She says that Dulcinea really was transformed into a peasant girl. Sancho tells the Duchess about his argument with her maidservant, Doña Rodriguez, and the Duchess vows to make sure that Dapple receives good care.

Chapter XXXIV
The Duke and Duchess go on a boar hunt with Sancho and Don Quixote. During the hunt, Sancho becomes afraid and attempts to climb a tree. The Duke tells Sancho that hunting helps to hone a governor's skill for warfare, but Sancho maintains his distaste for the sport. Suddenly the woods fill with the sound of drumbeats and Moorish battle cries. The devil appears to announce the coming of Montesinos, who will give instructions to Don Quixote about how to disenchant Dulcinea. The noises continue and three wagons drive by. The wagons, which carry demons, are drawn by oxen with torches on their horns. Each of the wagons contains an enchanter who announces himself and then drives on.

Chapter XXXV
An enormous wagon arrives carrying penitents dressed in white linen and a beautiful maiden with a golden veil. Merlin, bearing the face of death's head, also rides on the wagon and addresses Don Quixote in verse, telling him that to disenchant Dulcinea, Sancho must whip himself 3,300 times on his bare buttocks and that he must do it willingly. This news distresses Sancho, who says that Dulcinea's enchantment is not his problem. The maiden on the wagon, who pretends to be Dulcinea, chastises Sancho for his reluctance to come to her aid, and the Duke threatens to take away Sancho's governorship if he does not com-

ply. Sancho finally agrees but says that he will perform the whipping only when he feels like it. The scene pleases the Duke and the Duchess, who, it turns out, have arranged the whole trick in the first place.

ANALYSIS: CHAPTERS XXIX–XXXV

The Duke and the Duchess indulge Don Quixote's and Sancho's fantasies, validating both Don Quixote's belief that he is a grand knight-errant and Sancho's belief that he will gain a governorship by being a good squire. Through all of their trickery they exhibit their willingness to engage Don Quixote's madness. Don Quixote's imagination does not need to do much work to transform his stay at the Duke's castle into a magical one; it is the Duchess's imagination, not his, that drives most of his adventures there. Furthermore, the Duchess's indulgence of Sancho's high opinion of himself gives Sancho a chance to express his philosophy about life, which turns out to be quite wise and deeply rooted in Christian ideals of charity. By playing along with Don Quixote and Sancho rather than mocking them outright, the Duke and Duchess gain Don Quixote's and Sancho's trust. This trust gives them power over Don Quixote and Sancho, which they abuse to stage their elaborate ruse.

Cervantes uses the encounter at the castle to continue his critique of his era's conventional wisdom that social class corresponds to personal worth. Sancho is free to disagree with the lower-class Doña Rodriguez, but he is severely chastized by Don Quixote when he presumes to disagree with the Duke or the Duchess at dinner. According to the dictates of chivalry, Sancho, as a servant, may spar only with one of his own class. Likewise, Don Quixote treats the clergyman as roughly an equal, but he treats the Duke and the Duchess with the respect due to royalty. During their antics, the Duke and Duchess pretend that they are above everyone else, acting as puppeteers by stringing Don Quixote and Sancho along, tricking the men into believing each new fantasy simply for their own amusement. Though the Duchess does not appear overtly malicious, we see that she enjoys watching Sancho become more embroiled in Don Quixote's madness. The pleasure she takes is a symptom of her tendency to look upon the peasant squire with condescension, which compels us to disdain her. The Duchess begins to appear cruel, since she enjoys keeping Sancho in a confused and vulnerable position, most notably when she tells him to believe in the enchantment of Dulcinea despite the fact that it is clearly fake.

In highlighting the Duchess's awareness of the existence of the First Part of *Don Quixote,* Cervantes breaks down the wall between the work's factual and fictional components. The Duchess has knowledge of Don Quixote's past exploits, which shows that Cide Hamete Benengeli's so-called historical account has influenced the events and people Don Quixote encounters. Notably, Don Quixote himself has not read the novel, which accounts for his failure to understand the perhaps good-natured mockery of those who have read it. In essence, he fails to see himself the way other characters within the story see him. Cervantes implies that if only Don Quixote would pick up the book and begin reading his own story, he might respond differently to those around him. Because they have read the story, the Duchess and other characters later in the Second Part can share a joke with us. The result is dramatic irony, since we are aware of the joke while Don Quixote himself is not. This irony draws us deeper into the novel, further blurring the line between madness and sanity, truth and lies.

The Second Part, Chapters XXXVI–XLI

Chapter XXXVI
Sancho shows the Duchess a letter he wrote to his wife to tell her about his governorship. The Duchess shows the letter to the Duke over lunch. After lunch, to the sound of beating drums, a man appears, announces himself as Trifaldin of the White Beard, and requests that the Duke hear the plight of his maidservant. The Duke says he has heard about her misfortunes before and encourages her to come in.

Chapter XXXVII
Given his difficult history with the maidservants, Sancho fears that they will interfere with his governorship. Doña Rodriguez defends her profession and derides squires like Sancho. The Duke tells them to listen to Trifaldin's maidservant, who is hereafter referred to as the Countess.

Chapter XXXVIII
Cervantes says that Cide Hamete Benengeli briefly explains that the Countess Trifaldi's name—which means "the countess with the three skirts"—derives from her dress. Benengeli tells how she arrives accompanied by a dozen maids, all wearing black opaque veils. The Countess throws herself down before Don Quixote and begs his assistance, which he promises her. The Countess says she helped a knight at her king's court to gain access to the princess, whom she served as a maid. As a result, the princess got pregnant and had to marry the knight.

Chapter XXXIX
The Countess says that the princess's indiscretion so shocked her mother, the queen, that her mother died three days later. To punish the princess and the knight, the giant Malambruno turned the princess into a brass monkey and the knight into a metal crocodile on the queen's grave. Malambruno also posted a metal post between them with a note indicating that only Don Quixote can save them from their fate. Finally,

in return for the Countess's treachery, Malambruno gave her and all the other maids beards that cannot be removed.

CHAPTER XL

Don Quixote swears to avenge the Countess and the princess. The Countess tells him that the giant will send a flying wooden horse named Clavileño the Swift and that Don Quixote must fly on this horse to journey to her country that night to fight the giant. Sancho dislikes the idea of flying anywhere on a wooden horse, but the Duchess convinces him that he must go with his master.

CHAPTER XLI

> *Now that I've to be sitting on a bare board, does your*
> *worship want me to flay my bum?*
> (See QUOTATIONS, p. 80)

As the group waits in the garden, savages appears with a large wooden horse, which they deliver to Don Quixote with instructions that he blindfold himself and Sancho for the journey. Don Quixote pulls Sancho aside and asks him to whip himself a few hundred times to get started on the disenchantment of Dulcinea. Sancho, who dislikes the idea of riding on the back of a wooden saddle, refuses to whip himself.

The blindfolded Don Quixote and Sancho mount Clavileño the Swift and prepare to set off. At the last moment, Don Quixote, remembering the story of the Trojan horse, wants to check Clavileño's belly, but the Countess persuades him not to. Don Quixote turns a peg in Clavileño's forehead and they set off. The others blow wind in Don Quixote's and Sancho's blindfolded faces and bring fire near their heads to convince them that they are flying through the air and approaching the region of fire. The group then sets off firecrackers in Clavileño's belly, and the horse blows up, dumping Don Quixote and Sancho on the ground.

Upon waking, Don Quixote discovers that he and Sancho are still in the garden. Everyone else has fainted and lies on the ground nearby. They find a note on parchment paper saying that merely by attempting this feat, Don Quixote has accomplished it. The Countess has gone, and the Duchess and Duke tell them that she has embarked for home, happily beardless. Sancho tells the Duchess that he peeked as they flew and saw the earth no bigger than a mustard seed and that he played with the goats in heaven. Don Quixote says that since they could not have passed through the region of fire without being burned up, Sancho must be either lying about the goats or dreaming. But afterward, Don Quixote whispers in Sancho's ear that he will believe his story about the goats of heaven if Sancho will believe his story about Montesinos's Cave.

ANALYSIS: CHAPTERS XXXVI–XLI

In these chapters, Sancho's appealing simplicity contrasts with the distasteful actions of the Duke and Duchess. The incident with the Countess centers on Sancho's desire to be taken seriously. Overwhelmed by the opinions operating against him, by the desire for a governorship, and by his loyalty to Don Quixote, Sancho decides to brave the heights of heaven on a wooden horse to free others from their enchantments. Despite his unwillingness to whip himself, his courage makes him one of the novel's most sympathetic characters. We cannot tell whether Sancho is lying or dreaming when he tells the story about the goats of heaven, but, regardless, his story indicates his simple desire to live within the fantasy and receive his governorship. It is his simplicity—not an evil greediness—that motivates Sancho, which later makes his resigned attitude after the failure of his governorship touching.

Cervantes's sarcastic praise of Benengeli typifies his sarcastic praise of *Don Quixote*. Exalting over Benengeli's detail, Cervantes uses melodramatic phrases such as "O most renowned author!" which, in their sarcasm, imply a critical tone. Acting as both critic and author, Cervantes helps shape our experience of his work by interjecting editorial remarks and comments about the translation. He gives us two lenses through which to view his characters' actions—the lens of his characters' reactions and the lens of his own reactions. In so doing, he provides us with double vision—not just of the novel's factual and fictional elements but also of the work's quality. Cervantes can exalt Benengeli's descriptive ability at the times that his own descriptive ability is at its best. Cervantes excuses his own flights of fancy—as with the account of Montesinos's Cave—by allowing Benengeli to say that the manuscript from which he is working is dubious. This self-criticism contributes to the novel's ironic feel and self-referential tone.

Despite his occasional parodies of writers, in this section Cervantes completes his transition from a self-described historian into a masterful storyteller. We see his change in attitude in his choice of what to emphasize and what to downplay. In the First Part of the novel, Cervantes inserts chapter breaks whenever the characters sleep, and each chapter comprises a single encounter or a series of related encounters. Here, in shorter chapters, Cervantes inserts breaks according to the emotions in the scene. Whereas in the First Part he consistently ends each section with an explicit indication that some speech or incident will be finished in the next chapter, here he makes much less use of such guiding statements. Instead, he allows us to hear more frequently what the characters—both the main characters and the incidental ones—think about the events of the novel. In the Second Part, the main characters—especially Sancho—clearly develop, but even inconsequential characters such as Doña Rodriguez have rich personalities.

In essence, the Second Part reads like a traditional novel, rather than a parody of stilted chivalric tales.

THE SECOND PART, CHAPTERS XLII–XLVI

CHAPTER XLII
The Duke and Duchess, pleased with Don Quixote's and Sancho's reaction to the encounter with the Countess Trifaldi, send Sancho to his governorship right away. Sancho says he would rather have a piece of the sky than an isle, but the Duke says he can provide him only with an isle. The Duke and Duchess dress Sancho up and pack him off to a town, which he believes is an isle. Don Quixote gives Sancho advice on how to rule and reminds him never to be ashamed of his humble background. He also tells Sancho never to worry about injuring himself when confronting an enemy, to marry only a woman who will not take bribes, and to have pity and leniency on criminals.

CHAPTER XLIII
Don Quixote warns Sancho to refrain from eating garlic and onions, since only peasants eat such things; to walk slowly and speak deliberately; to eat little; not to drink too much; not to belch; and not to use so many proverbs. Don Quixote laments Sancho's illiteracy, but Sancho says he will prevent anyone from discovering this deficiency by pretending that his writing hand has been paralyzed. Sancho asks if Don Quixote thinks he will make a good governor, since he would rather just be Sancho than imperil his soul as a bad governor. Don Quixote assures him that he will be an excellent governor precisely because of this attitude.

CHAPTER XLIV
Cervantes interjects that "the real original history" claims that Cide Hamete Benengeli wrote this chapter in the form of a complaint addressed to himself for having written such a dry story and for not including as many digressions as he did in the First Part.

As he leaves for his governorship, Sancho mentions to Don Quixote that one of the stewards accompanying him looks and sounds exactly like the Countess Trifaldi, but Don Quixote dismisses Sancho's implication. After a sorrowful good-bye, Sancho sets out. Seeing that Don Quixote misses Sancho, the Duchess remarks that she has many maids who would gladly help cure Don Quixote's melancholy. Don Quixote refuses her offer and goes straight to bed after dinner, insisting on being alone to keep himself from temptation. Don Quixote hears two women under his window arguing about whether one of them, named Altisidora, should sing a ballad to the man she loves. Altisidora does sing the ballad, and Don Quixote concludes that she loves him. He laments his fate that no woman can see him and not fall in love. Meanwhile, Cervantes tells us that Sancho wishes to begin governing and awaits us.

CHAPTER XLV

The townspeople receive Sancho and set him up on the governor's chair, where they have written a proclamation that Don Sancho Panza took governorship on a certain date. Sancho has the proclamation read to him and then requests that no one call him "Don," since he is not a Don. He judges a series of cases, each involving some form of trickery, that the townspeople bring before him. Sancho resolves each case with wit and wisdom, impressing the town with his governing abilities.

CHAPTER XLVI

In the morning, Don Quixote passes Altisidora, who pretends to faint. He asks a servant to put a lute in his room that night so that he may disclose, in ballad form, his love for Dulcinea. Eager to play a trick on Don Quixote, Altisidora tells the Duke and Duchess about Don Quixote's plan. They all listen to his ballad to Dulcinea that night. As Don Quixote sings, one of the servants lowers a rope with bells on it and a bag of cats with bells on their tails onto the balcony above Don Quixote's window. The bells and the cats make a terrible noise, frightening Don Quixote and all those in the house. In the commotion, a couple of cats get into Don Quixote's room, and one of them jumps onto his face, bites his nose, and claws him. The Duke, who has rushed up to the room to see what is the matter, removes the cat. Altisidora tries to woo Don Quixote as she bandages his face.

ANALYSIS: CHAPTERS XLII–XLVI

In this section, Don Quixote and Sancho become intelligent and sensitive individuals when they are removed from situations involving chivalry. Don Quixote shows remarkable sense and compassion in his practical advice to Sancho about how to run his government, and Sancho demonstrates similar sense in his handling of the problems the townspeople send him. Despite his illiteracy, Sancho shows his remarkable ability to see through the Duke's tricks. Now distanced from Don Quixote for the first time since the end of the First Part, he does not attribute anything to enchantment or knight-errantry. Don Quixote does much the same: in contrast to his misinformed behavior toward Altisidora, his advice to Sancho concerning political matters is sensible and would serve a governor well.

Don Quixote's advice that Sancho not put on airs of good breeding—and Sancho's acceptance of this advice—stands in stark contrast to Don Quixote's need to play the role of the knight-errant. In effect, he tells

Sancho to be himself—a message that, on its surface, conflicts with everything we know about Don Quixote. The fact that Don Quixote has not read the historical account of his adventures—the First Part of *Don Quixote*—indicates that he does not wish to observe his actions from anyone else's perspective. Instead, he chooses to live a life of self-deception. At the same time, however, he never deceives others: unlike the Duke and Duchess and all those who exploit Don Quixote's madness in a belittling and insulting way, Don Quixote simply presents himself sincerely. His intentions are so exaggeratedly noble that, when he fears (erroneously) that Altisidora has fallen in love with him, he tries to make it clear that he is devoted to another woman in order to prevent future heartbreak for her.

The incident with the cats is the first of several events in which the Duke and Duchess's pursuit of self-amusement physically harms Don Quixote. What may appear at first to be a harmless prank becomes an insensitive and haughty act of cruelty. It is no longer possible to ignore the negative impact of the Duke and Duchess's lack of concern for others. Just as Don Quixote's inability to see the effect of his actions in the First Part nearly kills the farm boy, the Duke and Duchess here show no regard for Don Quixote's welfare. However, unlike Don Quixote, who would probably put an end to any plan he knew to be harmful, the Duke and Duchess compel Altisidora to woo Don Quixote even as she tends to his wounds. In this way, the two, who seem so kindly and courteous when we first meet them, slowly become the villains in this section.

THE SECOND PART, CHAPTER XLVII-LIII

CHAPTER XLVII
Sancho goes to dinner hungry on the first day on his alleged isle, only to discover that a physician there will not let him eat anything for fear that it might be bad for him. In a fury, Sancho threatens the physician and sends him out of the room. A courier then arrives with a letter from the Duke telling Sancho that he has learned about a plan to attack the isle and to kill Sancho. Sancho becomes convinced that the physician is one of the men threatening his life. A businessman arrives to ask Sancho for a letter of recommendation for his "bewitched" son (who likely suffers from autism) to marry the maimed, hunchbacked daughter of his neighbor. When the businessman also asks Sancho for six hundred ducats, Sancho flies into a rage and threatens to kill him.

CHAPTER XLVIII
In the middle of the night, Doña Rodriguez creeps into Don Quixote's room to ask him a favor. She tells Don Quixote the story of her daughter, who was wooed by a farmer's son who now refuses to marry her.

The Duke refuses to force the farmer's son to marry Doña Rodriguez's daughter, since the farmer is wealthy and the Duke does not want to risk losing the money he collects from the farmer. Don Quixote agrees to help Doña Rodriguez. She tells him that the Duchess has such a nice complexion because a physician drains the evil humors out of her legs. Doña Rodriguez's announcement shocks Don Quixote because he considers the Duchess an upright woman, but he admits that if Doña Rodriguez says it is true it must be so. At this point, someone rushes in and slaps and pinches both Doña Rodriguez and Don Quixote.

Chapter XLIX
Sancho encounters two criminal incidents on his rounds and then comes across a young girl dressed as a boy. The girl begins to cry, telling Sancho that her father, a widower, keeps her locked up day and night and never lets her see the world. She has switched clothes with her brother, she says, and snuck out to see the town because she is curious. As she tells her story, a guard catches her brother. Sancho takes them both home and tells them to be more careful next time.

Chapter L
The Duchess and Altisidora, Cervantes tells us, were listening outside Don Quixote's door to Doña Rodriguez's story about the Duchess's legs. It was the Duchess and Altisidora who ran in and pinched the two. The Duchess then sent a page to Teresa Panza to deliver Sancho's letter, along with a letter and a necklace of coral from the Duchess. Teresa receives the page and is thrilled by the news that her husband has been made a governor. She runs off to tell Sampson and the priest, who do not believe her until they speak with the page. Sampson offers to take dictation for Teresa's letter back to Sancho, but she does not trust him and goes to a friar to have him write it for her.

Chapter LI
The morning after his rounds, Sancho hears the petition of some judges who cannot decide whether to hang a man. The judges sit by a bridge whose owner demands that anyone wishing to cross must disclose his or her destination. If the person crossing tells the truth, he or she may pass, but if the person lies, he or she must be hanged on the gallows on the other side. A man has come to the bridge saying that he is going to be hanged on the gallows, which has confused the judges. If they set him free, then the man will be condemned by law to hang on the gallows, but if they hang him, then they must subsequently free him. Sancho sets the man free on the grounds that it is better to be too lenient than too strict.

Sancho receives a letter from Don Quixote that includes more advice about governing, along with the news that Don Quixote plans to do something that will anger the Duke and Duchess. Sancho replies with a long letter full of news, asking Don Quixote not to provoke the Duke and Duchess, since he does not want to lose his governorship. Sancho then makes the only laws he imposes during his governorship: a declaration that wine may be imported from anywhere as long as it clearly states its place of origin, along with a decree that he will lower the price of footwear, fix the wages of servants, and forbid the blind from singing about miracles unless the miracles are true. These laws please the populace so much, Cervantes says, that they still remain in effect and people call them "The Constitutions of the great Governor Sancho Panza."

CHAPTER LII

His wounds from his fight with the cats are now healed, and Don Quixote resolves to leave for the jousting tournament at Saragossa. Before he can ask the Duke's permission to leave, however, Doña Rodriguez and her daughter enter the great hall and throw themselves at Don Quixote's feet, begging him to avenge the wrong the farmer's son has done to them. Don Quixote promises to do so, and the Duke agrees to facilitate a duel.

The page returns from Teresa Panza with a letter for the Duchess and one for Sancho. The group reads both letters. The letter to the Duchess tells of Teresa's desire to go to court in a coach in order to do honor to her husband's name. Teresa also includes some acorns that she has harvested at the Duchess's request. Teresa's letter to Sancho rejoices in his success and tells some news about the village. The group applauds, laughs, and marvels at the letters.

CHAPTER LIII

In the middle of the night after his seventh day in office, Sancho hears cries of an attack on his isle. Playing a joke on him, his people urge him, against his will, to fight off the supposed enemies. They wrap him tightly between two shields and force him to begin marching, but he cannot march and falls to the ground, where they trample him. They then tell Sancho that they have prevailed against the enemy and praise him. But Sancho says that he must now abdicate his governorship, since he was never meant to lead. He says he will go tell the Duke of his decision, and he leaves on the back of his faithful Dapple.

ANALYSIS: CHAPTER XLVII-LIII

The incident with Doña Rodriguez and the conspiracy against Sancho further highlight the snobbery of the Duke and Duchess and, by contrast, exalt Don Quixote and Sancho for their magnanimity in the face of difficulty. While the Duke refuses to help the despairing Doña Rodriguez, even though she is his employee, Don Quixote gladly takes up her quest, making no distinction between her and the noble ladies he serves. The Duchess exhibits her nastiness by opening Sancho's mail with no concern for his privacy and not even delivering the letter to him until he leaves the castle for good, later in the Second Part. Sancho's mercy toward the man heading to the gallows contrasts with the Duke's contrived, pitiless assault on Sancho's "isle." The Duke and Duchess treat Don Quixote and Sancho as pawns—as characters in a play performed for their entertainment. The honorable and humble actions of Don Quixote and Sancho increases our distaste for those who treat them poorly.

The Panzas, for all their simplicity, turn out to be two of the wisest characters in the novel. Teresa warns Sancho not to wander too far from his God-given sphere—advice Sancho puts into action when he relinquishes his governorship. When the burden of office proves too much for him, Sancho gives it up without bitterness, longing to return to a better life as plain old Sancho. Teresa also shows sense and intuition in her distrust of Sampson, who does show himself to be untrustworthy. Sancho's laws—though they largely reflect the simplistic concerns of a peasant—prove so effective that they remain, according to Cervantes, codified in the town as "constitutions." Indeed, despite the Panzas' denseness and inscrutability, their proverbs are often more intelligent than the lofty but insincere words of Don Quixote. More important, the Panzas' wisdom sharply contrasts with the conniving actions of the Duke and the Duchess. Though the Duke and Duchess continue to mistreat the Panzas, the commoners rise above the pettiness of the nobles in their acts of sacrifice, discipline, and humility.

The puzzling situations of the townspeople create a diversion in the narration, much as the captive's tale and Anselmo's story do in the First Part. Like the stories in the First Part of the novel, these situations, such as the girl who dresses up as a boy in order to see the city and the indecisive judges at the bridge, are independent from the main story. But unlike in the First Part, Sancho now takes an active role in the situations he confronts. The situation of the indecisive judges at the bridge, for example, requires Sancho to identify and enact a solution. Nonetheless, these episodes feel strangely disconnected and fantastic, since they are very different from the issues a real governor would likely have to resolve. It is interesting to note that when faced with these more fantastical trials of governorship, Sancho performs very well and pleases his constituents. When faced with a more realistic trial, however, such as the attack on his governorship, Sancho is completely overwhelmed and unable to cope.

THE SECOND PART, CHAPTERS LIV–LX

CHAPTER LIV

The dishonorable lover of Doña Rodriguez's daughter, whom Don Quixote intends to fight, has fled the country. The Duke orders the lover's footman, Tosilos, to take his place in the duel against Don Quixote. Meanwhile, as Sancho and Dapple head toward the castle, they encounter a group of German pilgrims along with Sancho's old neighbor, Ricote the Moor, who left Spain when the king exiled the Moors. Ricote, who is on his way home to dig up some treasure he buried there, complains about his separation from his family during his exile. Sancho tells Ricote about his governorship, and Ricote asks what Sancho gained from his term in government. Sancho answers that he learned that he cannot govern anything but a herd of cattle.

CHAPTER LV

After leaving Ricote, Sancho and Dapple fall into a pit from which they cannot escape. Don Quixote finds them and gets others to help them out. Don Quixote and Sancho head back to the castle, where Sancho tells the Duke and Duchess about the end of his governorship. The Duke says he is grieved that Sancho has left his post as governor so soon but says that he will find Sancho a better position at the castle. The Duchess says she will have someone care for Sancho's badly bruised body.

CHAPTER LVI

On the day of the duel, the Duke removes the steel tips from the lances so neither of the combatants will be killed and takes several other measures to ensure a harmless fight. When Tosilos sees Doña Rodriguez's daughter, however, he falls in love and refuses to charge Don Quixote. Instead, he proposes to the daughter. Thinking that he is the farmer's son, she accepts but soon discovers the trick. Don Quixote assures the Duke that this transformation is nothing but the work of an evil enchanter, but the Duke, knowing the truth, locks up Tosilos.

CHAPTER LVII

Don Quixote and Sancho bid the Duke and Duchess farewell and Sancho happily receives Teresa's letters from the Duchess. As the pair starts to leave, however, Altisidora, pretending to be crushed that Don Quixote does not love her, utters a curse, in sonnet form, against him. She berates his cruelty to her and accuses him of stealing three handkerchiefs and a garter. But when the Duke questions her, she admits that she has the garter.

CHAPTER LVIII

On the road, Don Quixote and Sancho encounter some workmen carrying icons of saints to a nearby church. Don Quixote greatly admires the icons. In a wood beside the road, Don Quixote becomes entangled in some bird snares, which he mistakes for an evil enchantment. The two shepherdesses who set the snares appear and invite Don Quixote and Sancho to the new pastoral paradise they and others from their village are trying to create. Don Quixote declines the invitation but is very impressed. He vows to stand in the middle of the highway for two days, forcing everyone who passes to admit that these two shepherdesses are the most beautiful maids in the world after Dulcinea. Shortly after Don Quixote takes up his position on the road, however, a herd of bulls comes down the road. The herdsmen warn Don Quixote to step aside, but Don Quixote, Sancho, Rocinante, and Dapple are crushed.

CHAPTER LIX
Don Quixote and Sancho stop at an inn, which Don Quixote, for once, does not mistake for a castle. Eating supper, they encounter two gentlemen who have read the counterfeit sequel to the First Part of *Don Quixote*. Don Quixote exposes the book as a fake and the men criticize the book vehemently. Don Quixote also refuses to read the book, not wanting to give its author cause to gloat that people are reading it. When the two men tell Don Quixote that the false Don Quixote also traveled to Saragossa for a jousting competition, Don Quixote determines that he will never set foot in that town but will go to Barcelona instead.

CHAPTER LX
Sick of waiting for Dulcinea's disenchantment, Don Quixote tells Sancho he has decided to whip Sancho himself. The two argue. Sancho knocks Don Quixote down and, before letting him up again, makes Don Quixote swear he will not whip him. Don Quixote and Sancho then meet a band of thieves who robs them, although the thieves return the money at the command of their leader, Roque Guinart. Roque recognizes Don Quixote from the stories about him and says he never believed him to be real before now.

After a brief encounter with a distressed young woman who has killed her lover out of mistaken jealousy, Roque allows a group of wealthy individuals to keep most of their money, even giving some to two poor pilgrims traveling with them. Roque then kills one of his thieves for grumbling about his generosity. Roque sends a letter to a friend in Barcelona to alert him to Don Quixote's imminent arrival.

ANALYSIS: CHAPTERS LIV–LX
Don Quixote's encounter with the two men who have read the sequel to the First Part of the novel further blurs the line between fiction and reality. By this point, Don Quixote has begun to accept reality: he finally sees an inn as merely an inn and accepts that he must pay for his accom-

modations. Yet his return to reality comes just after the bulls crush him for standing his ground, an act that raises questions about his sanity. Still, he displays an ability to distinguish between the accurate First Part and the counterfeit sequel, refusing to read the sequel and disparaging its falsehood. Adding to the confusion is Don Quixote's refusal, in Chapter LIX, to go to Saragossa. At the end of the First Part, Cervantes tells us that the history indicates that Don Quixote goes to Saragossa on his next expedition. Now, however, it seems that Cervantes was either wrong or lying, since Don Quixote disobeys the very text in which his exploits are recounted.

As the novel draws toward its close, the status of the knight-errant declines, replaced by the virtue and strength of the peasant. When Sancho overpowers Don Quixote, Don Quixote's defeat and Sancho's evolution are nearly complete. Sancho the squire, who at the beginning of the novel would never even consider challenging his master's word, now physically knocks Don Quixote down without even apologizing, and even forces Don Quixote to swear an oath to him. Sancho's power and importance in the novel eclipse Don Quixote's literally trampled stature. At the same time, the chivalric qualities to which Don Quixote adheres so fiercely for so long have begun to lose their hold on him as he becomes a more practical and realistic—and compassionate and caring—human being.

The story of Tosilos, the lackey whom the Duke forces to fight Don Quixote for the Duke's amusement, is a glaring example of the Duke and Duchess's cruelty. The two combatants fight exclusively for the entertainment of two wealthy people who in their boredom are amused by the travails of the Countess and her dishonored daughter. Though the Duke takes steps to ensure that neither Tosilos nor Don Quixote will get hurt during the battle, he does not tell them that he has done so, because he wants to them to sweat and suffer as though they were in a real battle. Later, when we learn that Tosilos has been locked up for his refusal to fight and that Doña Rodriguez's daughter has been sent to a convent, the despicable nature of the Duke and Duchess becomes even clearer. Moreover, while the Duke and Duchess outwardly express grief for Sancho's troubled governorship, Cervantes writes about this grief with irony and doubts its sincerity. Though the Duke and Duchess claim to be upset at Sancho's "signs of having been badly bruised and worse treated," it is clear that Sancho does not merely have "signs" of bruises but that he *is* bruised. The Duke and Duchess meddle with their servants' lives merely for the sake of meddling, showing a clear enjoyment of power and a lack of compassion for others.

THE SECOND PART, CHAPTERS LXI–LXVI

CHAPTER LXI
Don Quixote and Sancho enter Barcelona with a great following as the guests of Roque Guinart's friends. A boy in town places burrs in Rocinante's and Dapple's tails, causing the two animals to throw their masters, much to the amusement of everyone but Don Quixote and Sancho.

CHAPTER LXII
Don Quixote and Sancho's host, Don Antonio Moreno, confides in Don Quixote that he owns an enchanted brass head that answers any questions asked of it. The next day, Don Quixote and Sancho parade around Barcelona with thousands of people following them. Don Antonio's men place a sign on Don Quixote's back that identifies him, and all the people of the town call to him. Don Quixote interprets their calls as proof of his fame. At a ball that evening, Don Quixote dances until he drops, and Sancho is embarrassed for him.

The next day, the brass head speaks to the guests via a hidden tube that allows a servant in the next room to hear and answer questions. Don Quixote asks the head whether the incident in Montesinos's Cave was real, and the head says that the incident was partly true and partly false. Don Quixote then asks whether Sancho will be whipped in order to disenchant Dulcinea, and the head answers that though Sancho's whipping will go slowly, Dulcinea's disenchantment will eventually be accomplished. Don Quixote then goes to a publishing house, where he discusses the art of translation with a translator and expresses his preference for histories that can be proved to be authentic.

CHAPTER LXIII
Don Quixote, Sancho, and Don Antonio visit the galleys. As a prank, the men hoist Sancho onto their shoulders and pass him around the ship. The ship amazes Sancho, who concludes that he must be either in hell or in purgatory. The galley captain spies a pirate ship in the distance, which they approach and stop. A skirmish ensues, and two of the galley soldiers die. Upon questioning, the captain of the Moorish pirate ship turns out to be a Christian woman, Anna Felix, who is an exiled Moor returning to Spain for a treasure her father buried before he left. Sancho's friend Ricote, a tourist on the ship, recognizes Anna, his daughter, and they embrace. Together, they invent a plan to save Anna's lover, Don Gregorio, who remains stranded in Moorish lands.

CHAPTER LXIV
Riding around one morning, Don Quixote encounters the Knight of the White Moon, who challenges Don Quixote and makes him swear to go

home and stay there for a year if he is defeated. Don Quixote agrees and the two fight. The Knight of the White Moon conquers Don Quixote but says that he will not defame Dulcinea's beauty. Don Quixote accepts the condition that he return home for one year.

Chapter LXV

Don Antonio and others desperately want to know the true identity of the Knight of the White Moon, so they follow him to an inn and pester him until he admits that he is Sampson Carrasco. Don Antonio chides Sampson for trying to bring Don Quixote back to his senses when people are deriving so much pleasure from his madness. Meanwhile, Don Gregorio, rescued from Algiers, returns to Barcelona, where he is happily reunited with Anna Felix.

Chapter LXVI

> *Great hearts, my dear master, should be patient in misfortune as well as joyful in prosperity.*
>
> (See QUOTATIONS, p. 80)

A forlorn Don Quixote departs Barcelona with Sancho, who urges his master to cheer up, saying that a good man should be patient in all things. Sancho suggests that they hang Don Quixote's armor in a tree, but he refuses, so Sancho places the armor on Dapple's back and walks. On the road, they encounter a group caught up in an argument. The group seeks Don Quixote's advice about a problem, but Sancho settles the problem with what the group considers a very wise decision.

Don Quixote and Sancho then encounter Tosilos. Tosilos says that just after they left the Duke's castle, he was flogged for not fighting Don Quixote, the Duke sent Doña Rodriguez back to Castile, and Doña Rodriguez's daughter became a nun. The news astonishes Don Quixote, who still believes that Tosilos is the farmer's son under an enchantment.

Analysis: Chapters LXI–LXVI

Don Quixote's fall from grace is complete when the Knight of the White Moon vanquishes him. This loss of glory is mirrored by Don Quixote's physical decline. Later, when he dies, he has returned to sanity but has largely lost his chivalric strength, as though his defeat at the hands of the Knight of the White Moon sapped his will to live. Don Quixote's psychological fall, however, truly intensifies at the ball the night before his defeat. Sancho's embarrassment over Don Quixote's collapse after dancing too much attests to the reversal of their roles of master and servant. The ball marks the last time that Don Quixote holds the upper hand over Sancho and the first time that Sancho acts paternally toward Don Quixote. Indeed, Don Quixote follows Sancho's lead for the rest of the novel, as we see when Sancho steps forward to settle the group's quarrel on the road home. Though the novel ends before we see how Sancho proceeds in life and what he does with his newfound identity, Cervantes does show that Sancho returns to his own home well-respected despite his humble social position.

The story of Anna Felix and Don Gregorio tempers Cervantes's otherwise rampant racism. From the outset, Cervantes mocks the Moors as liars and thieves, portraying them as useless cheapskates who deserve their exile from Spain because they threaten the king's rule. Even Cide Hamete Benengeli, the supposed author of the story, is a target of Cervantes's racism, since Cervantes blames all textual inconsistencies on Benengeli's lying Moorish nature. Much like Zoraida in the First Part, the character of Anna Felix challenges this stereotype of Moors, but only to a limited extent. Unlike her Spanish counterparts, Anna Felix is less scrutinized by Cervantes, presumably because he prejudicially considers her less than a true woman. Though Spanish society typically chastised women who dressed as men, Anna Felix, who is dressed as a young man, does not inspire such commentary from Cervantes. Despite the fact that Anna Felix is not the spitting image of a what Cervantes's readership would have considered ideal, she comes off as a respectable and sympathetic character, mellowing Cervantes's scathing attack on members of her race.

In general, however, determining whether the novel is prejudiced against the Moors is difficult. It is likely that Cervantes represents Spanish culture fairly—with the same amount of antagonism toward the Moors as toward others. But Cervantes explicitly claims that he is translating a Moorish manuscript, and when this manuscript is racist toward the Moors, we question why a Moor would be racist toward his own race. The various levels of narration and authorship depicted in the novel make it difficult to determine authorial intent.

THE SECOND PART, CHAPTERS LXVII–LXXIV

CHAPTER LXVII
Don Quixote implores Sancho to whip himself for Dulcinea's sake, but Sancho says he does not believe that his whipping will help Dulcinea. Don Quixote then decides to be a shepherd during his retirement, and he and Sancho begin to fantasize about their simple, pastoral lives.

CHAPTER LXVIII
Don Quixote wakes Sancho in the middle of the night to ask him again to whip himself, but Sancho again refuses. Sancho discourses on the nature of sleep, and Don Quixote marvels at Sancho's eloquence. Don Quixote quotes one of Sancho's own proverbs back to him, much to Sancho's astonishment. Some hogs that are being driven to a fair tram-

ple Don Quixote, Sancho, and Rocinante, but Don Quixote refuses to do battle with the hogs, believing instead that this trampling is punishment for his defeat at the hands of the Knight of the White Moon. Near dawn, ten horsemen ride up, capture the pair, and drive them to the Duke's castle.

Chapter LXIX

When the horsemen drag Don Quixote and Sancho into the Duke's courtyard, Don Quixote recognizes Altisidora on a funeral bier, apparently dead. The courtyard has been set up as a court, with the Duke, the Duchess, and two old judges, Minos and Rhadamanthus, sitting above the rest. A musician sings a poem—which Don Quixote recognizes as an adaptation of another poet's work—telling that Altisidora died out of her unrequited love for Don Quixote. Rhadamanthus demands that Sancho suffer a beating to bring Altisidora back to life. Sancho protests that he is tired of being beaten for Don Quixote's lovers. He nevertheless receives the beating, and Altisidora revives.

Chapter LXX

Cervantes says that Cide Hamete Benengeli tells how the Duke and Duchess were able to locate Don Quixote: on his way to defeat Don Quixote in the guise of the Knight of the White Moon, Sampson stopped at the Duke's house. Sampson knew that Don Quixote and Sancho had been staying there because he had been told so by the Duke's page, who had visited Teresa Panza to deliver Sancho's letter. Hearing that Sampson intended to end Don Quixote's career, the Duke and Duchess determined to have one last bit of fun and put the funeral sequence into action. Cervantes says that at this point, Benengeli declares that he considers the Duke and Duchess almost more mad than Don Quixote and Sancho for poking so much fun at such fools.

Altisidora comes into Don Quixote's bedroom and tells him about her bizarre trip to the gates of hell. She says she saw devils playing tennis and using books—including the false sequel to *Don Quixote*—for balls. The devils said that this false sequel should be thrown into hell. The musician from the night before appears, and Don Quixote asks him why he used another poet's work to describe Altisidora's situation. The musician answers that people commonly steal one another's literature in this age, calling the practice "poetic license." As Don Quixote and Sancho take their leave of the Duke and Duchess, Don Quixote recommends that Altisidora perform more chores so that she will not spend her days pining away for knights who do not love her.

Chapter LXXI

Don Quixote yet again suggests that Sancho whip himself, and Sancho again refuses. Don Quixote offers to pay Sancho, so Sancho goes into the woods and whips the trees so that his master will think he is whipping himself. The two then stop at an inn for the night, where Don Quixote muses about the paintings on the walls, hoping one day to be the subject of such paintings.

Chapter LXXII

While at the inn, Don Quixote and Sancho encounter Don Alvaro Tarfe, whom Don Quixote recalls from the false sequel. Don Alvaro admits that the false Don Quixote was his best friend but that the Don Quixote he sees now is the real Don Quixote. Don Alvaro swears to this account before the mayor, who records it. They stay overnight in the woods, where Sancho completes his whipping, still only whipping the trees.

Chapter LXXIII

As Don Quixote and Sancho enter their village, they hear two boys quarreling and a hare running from greyhounds. Don Quixote takes these sounds for bad omens, but Sancho disagrees. Sancho goes home to his family, while Don Quixote finds the priest, the barber, and Sampson. He tells them about his retirement and his plan to become a shepherd. They support his plan wholeheartedly. They also plan the jokes they will play on Don Quixote, despite the protests of the niece and the housekeeper, who want only to feed Don Quixote and put him to bed.

Chapter LXXIV

> *For me alone Don Quixote was born and I for him. His was the power of action, mine of writing.*
>
> (See QUOTATIONS, p. 81)

Don Quixote falls ill with a tremendous fever and lies in bed for six days, during which Sancho never leaves his side. When he wakes on the seventh day, Don Quixote has returned to sanity and recognizes that his real name is Alonso Quixano. He disavows all books of chivalry and repents his past actions. The priest, the barber, and Sampson come by and try to persuade him to pursue further adventures, especially the disenchantment of Dulcinea, but Don Quixote wants only to make his will. He leaves everything to his niece, his housekeeper, and Sancho. In his will, Don Quixote also tells his friends to ask the author of the false sequel to forgive him for providing the author with the occasion to write such nonsense. Don Quixote then dies.

Cide Hamete Benengeli mourns Don Quixote's passing, saying that he and Don Quixote were born for each other—Don Quixote to act, Benengeli to write. He adds that his sole purpose in writing was to rouse contempt for the "fabulous and absurd stories of knight-errantry."

ANALYSIS: CHAPTERS LXVII–LXXIV

Once Don Quixote renounces chivalry, he ceases to exist. After much digression on his way home, he unexpectedly has a bout of sanity and dies, as though the chivalric knight within him cannot live and breathe once he returns to a world whose values are different from his own. Don Quixote dreams for one night of being a shepherd and wakes a week later recanting everything that has come before—an act that may devalue many of the novel's adventures. Benengeli implies this devaluation when he writes about the dubious nature of the incident at Montesinos's Cave. Not even the apparently earnest attempts of Don Quixote's friends to make him rise and roam the countryside as a shepherd inspire him to live.

The meeting with Don Alvaro provides Don Quixote with one last chance to assert his identity. Already in a downward spiral, Don Quixote temporarily breaks out of his funk during this meeting. He asserts his dignity and former glory by repudiating the fake Don Quixote and by forcing the best friend of the fake Don Quixote to swear allegiance to him. Though this last-ditch effort to assert his honor may seem pathetic in light of his recent defeat by the Knight of the White Moon and his plans to retire, it displays Don Quixote's sincere nature.

The end of the novel is deeply concerned with authorship. The novel's conclusion abounds with insults against the counterfeit sequel to the history of Don Quixote. These insults include the remarks about the musician who justifies plagiarism, the tale of the devils who throw the book into hell, and Don Alvaro's disavowal of the counterfeit Don Quixote. Cervantes allows Benengeli to have the last word, which supports the idea that Cervantes has merely been translating Benengeli's text all along. At the end of the novel, Cervantes clings to his legacy as the bearer of Don Quixote's tale just as Don Quixote tries to preserve his name through Don Alvaro.

Even as Benengeli attempts to tear apart traditional chivalric texts, he elevates Don Quixote to an heroic status. Benengeli says that Don Quixote needed him to survive throughout history but adds that he needed Don Quixote in order to write. Cervantes's purpose in writing *Don Quixote* is much greater than simple self-glorification, a fact Cervantes highlights by distancing himself from the final words of the text. Benengeli admits that his purpose in writing was to show that chivalric tales are ridiculous, because they deny reality and gloss over the tragedy of trying to live an ideal, romantic life in an imperfect world. Benengeli wants his historical account of Don Quixote to put to rest any remaining chivalric tales that fail to highlight the tragic elements of knight-errantry—tragic elements so evident in the character of Don Quixote. Though Don Quixote's chivalric spirit and physical body may die, the final paragraph of the novel heightens our sympathy for Don Quixote, ensuring that he will live on with us.

IMPORTANT QUOTATIONS EXPLAINED

1.   [F]or what I want of Dulcinea del Toboso she is as good
as the greatest princess in the land. For not all those poets
who praise ladies under names which they choose so
freely, really have such mistresses. . . .I am quite
satisfied. . . to imagine and believe that the good Aldonza
Lorenzo is so lovely and virtuous. . . .

In this quotation from Chapter XXV of the First Part, Don Quixote explains to Sancho that the actual behavior of the farmer's daughter, Aldonza Lorenzo, does not matter as long as he can imagine her perfectly as his princess, Dulcinea del Toboso. This idea of Dulcinea figures prominently in the novel, since we never actually meet Dulcinea, and she likely does not even know about Don Quixote's patronage. Don Quixote's imagination compensates for many holes in the novel's narration, providing explanations for inexplicable phenomena and turning apparently mundane events into great adventures. Dulcinea gains renown through Don Quixote's praise, and regardless of whether she is even real, she exists in fame and in the imaginations of all the characters who read about her. In this way, Don Quixote's imaginings take on the force of reality and he becomes, effectively, the narrator of his own fate.

2.   I shall never be fool enough to turn knight errant. For I
see quite well that it's not the fashion now to do as they
did in the olden days when they say those famous knights
roamed the world.

In this passage from Chapter XXXII of the First Part, the innkeeper responds to the priest, who has been trying to convince him that books of chivalry are not true. Though the innkeeper defends the books, he says that he will never try to live like Don Quixote because he realizes that knight-errantry is outdated. The innkeeper's remark is important for several reasons. First, it inspires Sancho, who overhears the remark, to resolve—as he does at so many points throughout the novel—to return to his wife and children because knight-errantry has fallen out of fashion. The fact that Sancho does not leave Don Quixote becomes even more poignant when juxtaposed with his temptations to leave.

Second, this quotation highlights the priest's hypocritical nature. The innkeeper appreciates knight-errantry from a distance, but the priest, who plays the role of inquisitor against Don Quixote throughout much of the novel, cannot escape his fascination with knight-errantry. The priest furtively encourages Don Quixote's madness so that he may live vicariously through him.

3.   Now that I've to be sitting on a bare board, does your
      worship want me to flay my bum?

Sancho puts this question to Don Quixote in Chapter XLI of the Second Part, after Don Quixote suggests that Sancho whip himself to free Dulcinea from her alleged enchantment. With these words, which display his sarcastic wit, skepticism, and insubordinate nature, Sancho refuses to obey Don Quixote's order. The tale of Dulcinea's enchantment literally comes back to bite Sancho in the rear end—Sancho originally tells Don Quixote that Dulcinea is enchanted in an effort to hide the fact that he does not know where she lives and what she looks like. Sancho's lie nearly catches up with him a number of times until the Duchess finally snares him completely, telling him that Dulcinea actually *has* been enchanted. Sancho gullibly believes her story and later agrees to whip himself 3,300 times in order to revoke Dulcinea's enchantment. Nonetheless, Sancho is not happy with this course of action, and in the end he stands up to Don Quixote about it. This quotation not only fleshes out Sancho's character but also exemplifies the bawdy humor that pervades *Don Quixote*. Deeply ironic and complex, the novel is also very funny.

4.   Great hearts, my dear master, should be patient in
      misfortune as well as joyful in prosperity. And this I judge
      from myself. For if I was merry when I was Governor
      now that I'm a squire on foot I'm not sad, for I've heard
      tell that Fortune, as they call her, is a drunken and
      capricious woman and, worse still, blind; and so she
      doesn't see what she's doing, and doesn't know whom
      she is casting down or raising up.

Sancho's final words of wisdom to Don Quixote, which appear in Chapter LXVI of the Second Part, caution Don Quixote to be patient even in his retirement. Sancho's statement marks the complete reversal of his and Don Quixote's roles as servant and master. Throughout the novel, Don Quixote determines Sancho's role as a squire while teaching Sancho the chivalric philosophy that drives him. Now, however, Sancho consoles Don Quixote with the simple wisdom he has gained from his own experiences. Interestingly, Sancho still calls Don Quixote "dear master," even though he is no longer truly in Don Quixote's service.

Resigned to his humble station in life, he is not only simple and loyal but also wise and gentle.

5.   For me alone Don Quixote was born and I for him. His was the power of action, mine of writing.

These parting words of Cide Hamete Benengeli, in Chapter LXXIV of the Second Part, reflect Cervantes's words at the novel's beginning. At the start, Cervantes declares that Don Quixote is only his stepson—in other words, that he is not fully responsible for creating the character of Don Quixote. Don Quixote's real father, according to Cervantes's account, is Benengeli, the Moor from whose manuscript Cervantes claims to translate *Don Quixote*. Such remarks give the text a mythical, unreal tone that leaves us unsure whom to trust or to whom to attribute the story of Don Quixote. Additionally, the powerful sentiment that Benengeli expresses here contributes to the novel's claim that Don Quixote was a real person. Benengeli deemphasizes his role in bringing Don Quixote's story to light by casting himself as a mere recorder of a great man's life and deeds.

QUOTATIONS

KEY FACTS

FULL TITLE

The Adventures of Don Quixote

AUTHOR

Miguel de Cervantes Saavedra

TYPE OF WORK

Novel

GENRE

Parody; comedy; romance; morality novel

LANGUAGE

Spanish

TIME AND PLACE WRITTEN

Spain; late sixteenth and early seventeenth centuries

DATE OF FIRST PUBLICATION

The First Part, 1604; the Second Part, 1614

NARRATOR

Cervantes, who claims to be translating the earlier work of Cide
Hamete Benengeli, a Moor who supposedly chronicled the true
historical adventures of Don Quixote

POINT OF VIEW

Cervantes narrates most of the novel's action in the third person,
following Don Quixote's actions and only occasionally entering
into the thoughts of his characters. He switches into the first
person, however, whenever he discusses the novel itself or
Benengeli's original manuscript.

TONE

Cervantes maintains an ironic distance from the characters and
events in the novel, discussing them at times with mock seriousness.

TENSE

Past, with some moments of present tense

SETTING (TIME)

1614

SETTING (PLACE)

Spain

PROTAGONIST

Don Quixote

MAJOR CONFLICT

The First Part: Don Quixote sets out with Sancho Panza on a life of chivalric adventures in a world no longer governed by chivalric values; the priest attempts to bring Don Quixote home and cure his madness. The Second Part: Don Quixote continues his adventures with Sancho, and Sampson Carrasco and the priest conspire to bring Don Quixote home by vanquishing him.

RISING ACTION

The First Part: Don Quixote wanders Spain and encounters many strange adventures before the priest finds him doing penance in the Sierra Morena. The Second Part: Don Quixote wanders Spain and has many adventures, especially under the watch of a haughty Duke and Duchess.

CLIMAX

The First Part: Don Quixote and the priest meet in the Sierra Morena, and Dorothea begs for Don Quixote to help her avenge her stolen kingdom. The Second Part: Sampson, disguised as the Knight of the White Moon, defeats Don Quixote.

FALLING ACTION

The First Part: the priest and the barber take Don Quixote home in a cage, and Don Quixote resigns himself to the fact that he is enchanted. The Second Part: Don Quixote returns home after his defeat and resolves to give up knight-errantry.

THEMES

Perspective and narration; incompatible systems of morality; the distinction between class and worth

MOTIFS

Honor; romance; literature

SYMBOLS

Books and manuscripts; horses; inns

FORESHADOWING

Cervantes's declaration at the end of the First Part that there will be a second part and that Don Quixote will die in it, coupled with the niece's and the housekeeper's fear that Don Quixote will run away again, hints at Don Quixote's fate in the Second Part.

STUDY QUESTIONS & ESSAY TOPICS

STUDY QUESTIONS

1. *How does Don Quixote's perception of reality affect other characters' perceptions of the world? Does his disregard for social convention change the rules of conduct for the other characters?*

In many ways, *Don Quixote* is a novel about how Don Quixote perceives the world and about how other characters perceive Don Quixote. His tendency to transform everyday people and objects into more dramatic, epic, and fantastic versions of themselves forces those around him to choose between adapting to his imaginary world or opposing it. Some, such as the barber and the priest, initially try to coax Don Quixote back into a more conventional view of the world and away from his unconventional life as a knight-errant. To get Don Quixote to communicate, however, they must play along with his world, pretending to believe in his wild fantasies. By the end of the novel, these characters achieve a more harmonious relationship with Don Quixote's fantasy world, recognizing its value even if they do not believe it is literally true.

Those who oppose Don Quixote—namely, Sampson Carrasco and the Duke and Duchess—find their lives disrupted by Don Quixote's perceptions of the world. Sampson temporarily becomes a knight to seek vengeance on Don Quixote, sacrificing his own perceptions of the world because he is obsessed with altering Don Quixote's world. The Duke and Duchess find that the people and events around them actually match Don Quixote's vision much more closely than they expected, as adventures such as Sancho's governorship and the adventure of Doña Rodriguez fit well into Don Quixote's world and not so well into their own.

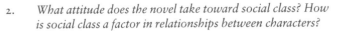

2.   *What attitude does the novel take toward social class? How*
      is social class a factor in relationships between characters?

The differences between social classes operate on many levels throughout *Don Quixote*. The novel emphasizes Sancho's peasant status, the Duke and Duchess's aristocratic status, and Don Quixote's own genteel upbringing. But the novel does not mock any one class more than the others: Sancho's peasant common sense makes noblemen appear foolish, but his ignorance and lack of education make *him* appear foolish just as often. Furthermore, Don Quixote almost invariably sees beyond the limiting boundaries of social class to the inner worth of the people he meets. His good nature typically leads him to imagine that people are of higher social classes than they actually are—prostitutes become ladies, innkeepers become lords, and country girls become princesses.

Social class in the novel often appears as an impediment to what a character truly wants. Most of the pairs of lovers in the novel, for instance, must overcome difficulties of class difference to achieve their love. Only through disguises, tricks, and acts of imagination can characters overcome their social circumstances and act according to their true values.

3.   *Like Hamlet's madness, Don Quixote's insanity is the subject*
      of much controversy among literary critics. Is Don Quixote
      really insane, or is his behavior a conscious choice? What
      might account for the change in his behavior over the course
      of the novel?

Early in the novel, Don Quixote seems completely insane, failing to recognize people and objects, wantonly attacking strangers, and waking up in hallucinatory fits. As the novel progresses, however, this madness begins to seem more a matter of Don Quixote's own choosing. He occasionally implies to his friends that he knows more than they think he does. Moreover, he often tries to fit his madness into the forms of behavior prescribed by books of chivalry, as when he meticulously plans out his penance in the Sierra Morena. In the Second Part, whenever Don Quixote feels melancholy or dissatisfied with his life as a knight-errant, his behavior becomes much more sane, and he fully controls his own actions. Near the end of the novel, he spends an entire chapter describing to Sancho what their shepherd life will be like—essentially planning out a new form of madness—and seems to be completely sane. When he finally dies, it is as his real self, Alonso Quixano.

There are several possible interpretations for what appears to be Don Quixote's gradual recovery of sanity over the course of the novel. The simplest explanation may be that Don Quixote is insane in the beginning and his condition slowly improves. Second, it could be that, in his first passionate burst of commitment to knight-errantry in the First Part, he acts more rashly than he needs to and eventually learns to regulate his eccentric behavior. Alternatively, it could be that Don Quixote is consistently sane from the beginning and that Cervantes only slowly reveals this fact to us, thereby putting us in the same position as Don Quixote's friends, who become aware of his sanity only by degrees. Or it could be that Cervantes began his novel intending Don Quixote to be a simple, laughable madman but then decided to add depth to the story by slowly bringing him out of his madness in the Second Part. Finally, it must be remembered that Cervantes never gives us a verdict on Don Quixote's mental health: despite the evidence, the question is still open to interpretation.

SUGGESTED ESSAY TOPICS

1. Throughout *Don Quixote,* Cervantes claims that his novel is a true history about real people and based on documented evidence. Why does he make this claim? How do his games with history and authorship advance the themes of the novel?

2. Many characters in *Don Quixote* serve as foils, or opposites, of other characters. What role do these opposed pairs play in developing the novel's themes?

3. What is the role of parody in *Don Quixote?* How does the novel mock books of chivalry, and how does it defend them? Do the characters who mock and try to humiliate Don Quixote come across in a positive or a negative light?

4. *Don Quixote* highly values genuine romantic love, yet many of the love stories embedded in *Don Quixote* are resolved only through trickery. What is Cervantes implying if true love in the novel can be realized only by deceit?

5. How would you characterize each of Don Quixote's three expeditions? What is the significance of having three expeditions rather than one long expedition? How do the two parts of the novel differ?

REVIEW & RESOURCES

QUIZ

1. Who is the Knight of the White Moon?

    A. The Duke
    B. Cardenio
    C. Sampson Carrasco
    D. Sancho Panza

2. How many expeditions does Don Quixote make without Sancho Panza?

    A. None
    B. One
    C. Two
    D. Three

3. Why does Don Quixote return home in a cage after his second expedition?

    A. Because he believes he is enchanted and cannot get out
    B. Because Benengeli has vanquished him
    C. Because Dorothea asks him to
    D. Because he wants to

4. Who is Master Peter, the puppeteer?

    A. Don Quixote
    B. Ferdinand
    C. Anselmo
    D. Gines de Pasamonte

5. Where does Don Quixote meet the enchanted Dulcinea for the second time, after meeting her once on the road to El Toboso?

    A. The Duke's house
    B. Barcelona
    C. In heaven
    D. In Montesinos's Cave

6. How does the Duchess know who Don Quixote and Sancho Panza are?

    A. From reading about them in the First Part of the novel

    B. From her servants, whom they conquered on the road

    C. From an oracle in La Mancha

    D. From the Countess Trifaldi

7. Why does Don Quixote do penance in the Sierra Morena?

    A. Because he is insane

    B. Because he lied to Dulcinea

    C. Because his hero, Amadis of Gaul, performed a similar penance

    D. Because of his guilt over stealing Mambrino's helmet from the barber

8. What does Anselmo ask his best friend, Lothario, to do for him?

    A. Take care of Anselmo's ailing sister

    B. Seduce Anselmo's wife

    C. Carry a message to Don Quixote

    D. Take Anselmo's wife to a nunnery

9. When he sees them, what does Don Quixote think the fulling mills are?

    A. Windmills

    B. Giants

    C. Castles imprisoning a famous knight-errant

    D. Fulling mills

10. Who is Cide Hamete Benengeli?

    A. Don Quixote's grandfather

    B. The captive's Moorish captor

    C. Countess Trifaldi's enchanter

    D. The author, according to Cervantes, of the manuscript from which Cervantes translates *Don Quixote*

11. What does the Duke give Sancho Panza?

    A. A horse

    B. An "isle"

    C. A kiss

    D. A whipping

12. How, according to Merlin, can Dulcinea be released from her enchantment?

   A. If Sancho gives himself 3,300 lashes with a whip on his bare bottom
   B. If she touches Don Quixote
   C. If she wears Mambrino's helmet
   D. If she drinks the Balsam of Fierbras

13. Why do the officers of the Holy Brotherhood want to arrest Don Quixote?

   A. For knocking over the windmills
   B. For beating up the penitents
   C. For refusing to pay his bill at the inn
   D. For releasing the galley slaves

14. Who is Cardenio?

   A. The crazy naked man in the Sierra Morena
   B. Lucinda's lover
   C. Dorothea's friend
   D. All of the above

15. What does Countess Trifaldi have that she does not want?

   A. Money
   B. 100 suitors
   C. A giant enslaving her kingdom
   D. A beard

16. Who pretends to be Princess Micomicona?

   A. Lucinda
   B. Dorothea
   C. The priest
   D. The Duke's steward

17. How does Sancho prove that Don Quixote is not actually enchanted in the cage?

   A. By asking him if he needs to go to the bathroom
   B. By showing that his armor is undamaged
   C. By getting in the cage with him
   D. By breaking the cage

REVIEW & RESOURCES

18. Who wrote the false Second Part of *Don Quixote*, in which Don Alvaro brings Don Quixote to be cured?

    A. Cervantes
    B. Avellaneda
    C. Cide Hamete Benengeli
    D. Sancho

19. How does Don Quixote die?

    A. The Balsam of Fierbras poisons him
    B. The Knight of the White Moon kills him
    C. Robbers kill him outside Barcelona
    D. He falls ill

20. Why does Sancho whip the trees?

    A. Because he wants to save Dulcinea
    B. Because he hates forests
    C. Because he wants to trick Don Quixote into thinking that he is actually whipping himself
    D. Because he is jealous of Don Quixote's romantic success with the innkeeper's daughter

21. Why does Cervantes end the First Part?

    A. He runs out of paper
    B. Sancho dies
    C. His translator runs away
    D. He does not know the rest of the story

22. Why does Sancho *not* take Don Quixote to Dulcinea's house at the beginning of the Second Part?

    A. He does not know where Dulcinea lives
    B. He does not want to bother Dulcinea at night
    C. He is afraid of the demon guarding Dulcinea's gate
    D. He is tired and wants to go to an inn

23. When *during the novel* does Don Quixote see Dulcinea for the first time?

    A. When Sancho brings her to him in the Sierra Morena
    B. When he goes to El Toboso
    C. When he goes home at the end
    D. He never sees her during the course of the novel

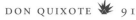

24. What does Don Quixote decide to do during his retirement?

    A. Hunt
    B. Fish
    C. Tend sheep
    D. Read

25. Why does Don Quixote sing to Altisidora?

    A. To prove that he loves her
    B. Because the Duchess has asked him to
    C. To prove that he does not love her
    D. Because she is afraid of him

SUGGESTIONS FOR FURTHER READING

BELL, AUBREY. *Cervantes*. Norman: University of Oklahoma Press, 1947.

CANAVAGGIO, JEAN. *Cervantes*. J.R. Jones, trans. New York: W.W. Norton & Company,1990.

EL SAFFAR, RUTH, ed. *Critical Essays on Cervantes*. Boston: G.K. Hall, 1986.

JOHNSON, CARROLL. *Cervantes and the Material World*. Urbana: University of Illinois Press,2000.

MANCING, HOWARD. *The Chivalric World of DON QUIJOTE: Style, Structure, and Narrative Technique*. Columbia: University of Missouri Press, 1982.

PERCASE DE PONSETI, HELENA. *Cervantes the Writer and Painter of DON QUIJOTE*. Columbia: University of Missouri Press, 1988.

PRESBURG, CHARLES. *Adventures in Paradox: DON QUIXOTE and the Western Tradition*. University Park: Pennsylvania State University Press, 2001.